THE SOCIABLE CAT

Building harmonious relationships for your cat and family

Melissa Fallon & Becky Macfarlane

The Hubble & Hattie imprint offers a range of books that cover all things animal, promoting compassion, understanding and respect between all animals (including humans!)

Some more great books from Hubble & Hattie!

Also in this series:

Babies, Kids and Dogs (Fallon & Davenport)
Life Skills for Puppies (Zulch, Mills and Baumber)
Helping Minds Meet (Zulch/Mills)
Home alone and happy! (Mallatratt)

A Masterclass in Needle Felting (Series: Dogs; Wildlife; Endangered Species) (Thompson)
Cat and Dog Health, The Complete Book of (Hansen)
Fun and Games for Cats (Seidl)
Unleashing the healing power of animals: True stories about therapy animals – and what they do for us (Preece-Kelly)
Wildlife photography from the edge (Williams)
Wonderful Walks from Dog-friendly Campsites (Series: Throughout the UK; With Dog-friendly Pubs Nearby; On a Budget) (Chelmicka)

www.hubbleandhattie.com

First published 2025 by Hubble & Hattie, an imprint of David & Charles Ltd, c/o Veloce office: 2 Poundbury Business Centre, Middle Farm Way, Poundbury, Dorchester, DT1 3WA England. Tel 01305 260068 / e-mail info@veloce.co.uk.

ISBN: 9781836440079

Front cover images: Main and lower left images licensed for use by Adobe Stock; other three small images AI-generated by Adobe Stock.

British Library Cataloguing in Publication Data – A catalogue record for this book is available from the British Library. Typesetting, design and page make-up by Hubble & Hattie, an imprint of David & Charles.

Printed in Turkey by Pelikan Printing.

Contents

Introduction

Cats have always been one of the most popular pets, second only to dogs. Around a quarter of homes in the UK have at least one cat as part of the family, with the family dynamics being remarkably varied. We see our cats living in multi-cat and multi-pet households, as well as being an important part of many a childhood.

Cats often live harmoniously and even benefit from living with other cats, dogs and children. Living within these environments can help build their confidence, resilience and adaptability, however it is important that we set them up for success. Where possible we should be selecting the right individuals, preparing them and the environment effectively, and then integrating them slowly and in the most successful manner. This book aims to provide practical guidance on how to introduce cats to other cats, to dogs and to children, to safely create harmony within the family, as well as improve current relationships within the home. This guidance also aims to reduce the likelihood of relinquishment by increasing knowledge and improving success, in a bid to help the unowned cat crisis faced by rescue centres.

For ease of reading, the text refers to the cat as she/her throughout the book, while the dog will be referred to as he/him in chapter four, and children will be referred to as they/them in chapter five, however no gender bias is implied and advice remains the same regardless of gender.

1: Cats in our community

Cats have had several roles in human society throughout history, and have become integrated into our homes. This chapter is going to discuss how cats have adapted to live amongst people, whether that is in feral communities or in our homes. We will also consider the 'inbetweener' cats, and discuss our perceptions and expectations of the cats that live with us. Finally, some of the main welfare concerns for cats will be highlighted, we'll also examine their needs and how their welfare can be improved.

1.1 The domesticated cat

The domestication of cats began in the Middle East between 10,000 and 12,000 years ago, and our domestic cats today share a common ancestor: the North African wildcat. Cats are very intelligent and will adapt their behaviour so that they are successful in the environment in which they live. These survival adaptations allow them to maintain their physical health by gaining and maintaining access to desirable resources and spaces.

Domestication arose from cats being attracted to early agricultural communities, where they preyed on the rodents that were attracted to grain stores. The cats became more accustomed to people over time, and has resulted in their roles in society becoming more diverse, including as companions and in therapy roles. There is still contention as to whether cats are truly domesticated at all, predominantly based on their well-retained wild characteristics and behaviours. It is also the case that not all domestic cats are considered pet cats, some come under the umbrella of feral/inbetweener cats, which further blurs the domestication line. Cats' roles in society are determined by their level of sociability, adaptation to a domestic home, and their desire to live with people. These cats are all genetically the same species, *Felis catus,* but their behaviour is somewhat varied. International Cat Care has produced a clear visual that looks at where cat types fit on a sociability spectrum; this can be seen in Figure 1.1.

Feral and free-living cats

As seen, a feral cat is one that has adapted to free-living and has no desire to live with people. Cats are generally selectively social animals, and in free-range conditions feral cats tend to live in larger groups known as colonies, made up of mostly several related female adults and their litters. Multiple generations of related females can live together, allowing for communal rearing of kittens, giving kittens access to multiple lactating queens, as well as the provision of killed or disabled prey that will be distributed indiscriminately among all kittens, regardless of which female they belong to. Offspring reach sexual maturity at around six months old, and tend to stay within their social group until around 12-18 months old. Young males are more frequently pushed out of the colony to prevent close relative inbreeding.

Breeding between feral cats can be indiscriminate but evidence has shown that females are more likely to avoid copulation with close kin, although not with distant relatives. This reduces the chance of inbreeding and therefore associated genetic and health problems that come with close relative breeding.

The Sociable Cat

Figure 1.1. International Cat Care spectrum of the domestic cat. (© International Cat Care)

Free-living (feral) cats seem to be somewhat flexible in their social grouping. The size of a colony is very much dependent on the space and concentration of resources available, particularly food and suitable resting and nesting sites. Cats are solitary hunters that hunt predominantly rodents and other small animals. Many feral colonies are situated close to smallholdings and farms due to the abundance of food items and shelter. One of the key reasons they have co-existed with people so successfully is their ability to control what we consider vermin, and feral cats are still 'recruited' to remove populations of rodents from a range of settings. Their role in society is solely linked to their role as predators, and feral cats should not be housed as pets as this will significantly impact their behaviour and welfare.

Feral kittens under eight weeks old can generally be socialised appropriately enough to be placed into homes as pets, with very little impact on their welfare as they mature. Feral kittens above the age of eight weeks should not be housed with the intention to socialise and re-home as a pet cat. The key socialisation period has passed and there can be negative welfare consequences when attempting to 'tame' such individuals. The best outcome for those trapped above eight weeks is to neuter them, and return or release to a secure site with caregivers who are prepared to provide shelter, food and basic care, whilst maintaining respect and a hands-off approach.

Other cats fit under the 'free-living' (street/community) or 'inbetweener' categories, and these have a mixture of traits and behaviours from both pet cats and feral cats. Inbetweener cats are considered cats who have once been pets but are now free-living for whatever reason, perhaps abandoned by their owner. Street cats are individuals that have spent their lives living free of a domestic household, but are not considered feral, and do not belong to a colony. These cats do have some sociability with humans and therefore can sit within a spectrum of their own when it comes to individual sociability with humans. Many will be able to adapt back to living in homes with close human contact, whereas others will prefer to keep a distance from humans, and will continue to live independently outdoors. A key point regarding these individuals is that they do require care and maintenance by caregivers to ensure sufficient welfare. Provision of food, veterinary care, and medicines when required will improve their overall quality of life.

Cats in our homes

Domestic cats have adapted to successfully live within our homes: their communication skills have adapted, they have become more sociable, and have adapted to life within our families, becoming resilient to some of the restrictions in our society. Their level of sociability is still dependent on the individual, but their behaviours towards humans and life within a home are significantly more positive than those of feral and free-range cats.

Breeding has an impact on both behavioural traits and suitability as cats in our homes. Queens are 'induced ovulators', meaning they require breeding to release eggs, and therefore need multiple copulations to become pregnant. Their cycle is generally seasonal (most often from winter to summer), about every three weeks if not bred. Litter size ranges from two up to nine in some oriental breeds, with litters of four being most common. Weaning occurs at around 5-8 weeks old, although there is some variation with some kittens suckling much later; however, this is thought to be more social than nutritional. Those who are removed from their mother prior to weaning or before its completion can lead to kittens with an earlier onset of play and predation behaviours.

Unneutered cats have significant focus on reproduction and therefore will display behaviours which many find undesirable and 'problematic.' Unneutered cats also cause problems in society, especially with regards to the general overpopulation and impact on welfare. For this reason, it is always recommended to neuter cats over the age of four months if pets, and from eight weeks if feral. Neutering will reduce, if not eliminate, some of the undesirable behaviours such as fighting, calling and spraying, and therefore leads to more harmonious relationships and interactions all round.

Pet cats can live in a variety of environments, and are exposed to a range of interactions with people and other animals. Cats are good at distinguishing between individuals, and close bonds can be formed with caregivers, whilst still being able to retain their independent nature. Cats generally don't have the same attachments to their humans as dogs do, and certainly don't rely on them to the same level. We do, however, still hold the resources they require, and pet cats have developed ways to manipulate access to those resources.

It is well known that the cat's meow has adapted over time to be around and communicate with humans. Feral and free-living cats have much-reduced instances of vocal communication, such as meows, compared with pet cats, especially in adult cats. Pet cats have developed a complex form of communication for humans and other pet cats, with caregivers often able to distinguish their own cats' meows and the context in which they are communicating. This shows a clear adaptation to cats communicative behaviour that assists in developing strong relationships with humans

1.2 Our perceptions and expectations of cats

Perceptions and expectations are concepts as to how we interpret experiences and how we interact with the world around us. **Perceptions** link to the way people interpret information and experiences in the past or present, and these can be shaped by belief systems and cultural backgrounds. For this reason, perceptions are subjective, with two people perceiving an event entirely differently based on their experiences and even emotional states. **Expectations** are linked to the future and us anticipating what may occur, based on our previous experiences and what is expected in society. Expectations can influence how we behave and the decisions that we make.

Perceptions of cats

Historically, humans have perceived cats in many ways in different cultures, both in positive and negative ways. Traditional views on cats in society have varied: in many parts of the world, including Africa, Asia and Europe, they have been a source of food; elsewhere they were considered sacred or had gods based on their form, as in Ancient Egypt (known as Mau and associated with the goddesses Isis and Ba'at); they may be considered a sign of prosperity, as with the lion-cats in China; and black cats have traditionally been seen as both a sign of bad luck, such as in the USA and Europe, and good luck, such as in Japan and Russia. The city of Imabari in Japan has a small cat shrine (neko jinja) dedicated to the protection of cats, and has an association with 'lucky cats', traditional Japanese talismans which are believed to bring good fortune. Tashirojima island is known as 'cat island', famous for its large population of stray cats which are cared for by its residents.

Perceptions have also changed historically, during the Middle Ages in Europe, Vikings used cats to catch rats, and the Medieval King of Wales made legislation to make it illegal to kill or harm cats. In contrast, cats were also associated with witches, as their familiars, and killed en-masse, particularly during the time of the Black Death, and during festivities were burnt alive or thrown off tall buildings. Perceptions eventually came full circle and cats became popular again, with sympathetic characters created in such folk tales as Puss in Boots.

In the present day our perceptions vary depending on the role they play within our society. In some locations, such as China, Vietnam and Korea, cats are still a source of food for some minority groups. Opinions on the practice are emotionally charged; many are now opposing the tradition, and it is becoming less common. Cats can also be seen as a pest by home and landowners, particularly regarding free-ranging cats and feral colonies; they are also seen as a conservation threat by some, particularly regarding songbirds and small mammal species. On the other hand, they are seen as excellent companions and are also used as therapy animals; providing comfort and companionship in a range of settings from private homes to schools and healthcare facilities. As companions they are thought to develop close bonds and attachments with them and are viewed by many as being important members of the family. Where they may be viewed as a food source in some areas, in others, such as Egypt, they are still seen as sacred. Cats, more specifically feral cats, are also frequently used to control the number of rodents and other pests from small-holdings and farmland; and they are seen as a source of entertainment across a range of media.

Perceptions can also link to a cat's behaviour, with cats having had a long history of being considered independent and aloof, which are generally viewed as negative traits. Those who have had positive experience with cats, however, may describe them as affectionate, playful and loyal.

Expectations of cats

Our expectations of cats vary between households, however generally we expect them to be quite resilient and adaptable. We expect cats to be able to cope with changes to their environment and/or routine, deal with a variety of household objects and noises, live alongside other animals (even if just tolerating them), be transported in carriers, deal with restrictions in their environment (access to resources such as going outside), moving house, changes to household members, and more. We expect cats to adapt to these many changes and behave in a calm manner, whilst also showing resilience by bouncing back from any changes and adjustments quickly and without long-term effects.

We may also have the same expectations of each cat we have, without taking into consideration their individual differences. If we have had cats in the past which have been sociable and steady, we expect our future cats to behave in the same way. When this doesn't happen due to individual differences and experiences, this leads to frustration and misunderstanding, which can impact our relationships. We have all these expectations of our pet cats, regardless of their genetics, sociability or general experiences, and often without providing any extra support or input.

It was previously mentioned how our perception of cats is often as aloof, independent creatures, and this can influence how much involvement or input we feel we need to have in their lives. This is evidence of the general lack of understanding or appreciation we have for their natural behaviour, and how us as humans have a significant part to play in their wellbeing, whether they were historically considered independent or not. We now know better, so can do better in our approach to their care and overall welfare.

1.3 Welfare considerations

There are a range of factors which should be encompassed when welfare is considered; from basic care and the environment to the holistic physical and emotional needs of each cat as an individual. We must consider how any adjustments or restrictions can impact these needs, and be aware of and acknowledge what we can do to further promote welfare.

Predictability and routine

Cats are well known for their love of routine and predictability within their daily schedule. Instances where routine changes or activities are unexpected can cause a level of stress in our pet cats which may lead to problematic behaviours or a change in expected behaviour. Predictability provides stability for our pet cats, a species which relies heavily on territoriality and clear social boundaries to prevent conflict. A stable environment provides our cats with a sense of control and comfort, something which is important; especially when many elements of their life are taken out of their control daily.

Feeding schedule: Ensuring cats are fed at the same time of day is one of the easiest ways of maintaining a sense of routine. Food predictability can remove any elements of stress or frustration which may be apparent if feed times are unpredictable or not known. A feeding schedule can also support weight management, by ensuring cats who need their diet controlling or monitoring in some way have set feeding times.

Environmental stability: Keeping the environment as consistent as possible is also a way of maintaining predictability. Temperature will fluctuate naturally, but it is possible to control the parameters of this through use of equipment, for example heat pads or fans. Noise is also likely to fluctuate regularly throughout the day depending on how busy a household is, but routine plays a part here whereby cats will be able to predict when events will occur and act accordingly. For example, a household with young children may be relatively quiet between the hours of 9am and 3pm, but peak between the hours of 7am to 8.30am and again at 3.30pm to 7pm. This daily routine is predictable for our cats, and therefore has minimal impact on welfare.

Caregiver responses: The responses we provide to our cats when they perform certain behaviours or tasks are also predictable. Whether they are vocalising for food, nuzzling us for attention or tapping on cupboards or doors, our responses are noted and therefore expected each time the behaviour is performed when responses are consistent. If our response is not as expected by our felines, this can lead to frustration and then potential undesirable behaviour being exhibited.

Space

Space is an important factor with regards to all species, and our felines are no different. It is the quality of the space that is of most importance however, rather than the amount provided. There is most debate regarding outdoor access provision for our pet cats, and, whilst this book does not aim to address this ethical dilemma, it does factor in the need for space provision. There is no specific space requirement outlined for cats as such, certainly not in the same manner as we see for some of our smaller companions, such as rodents and rabbits, who are confined. Space is, however, an aspect of upholding the welfare needs of our pet cats and should be thoroughly considered when looking at the environment. Space can be achieved if any of the cats are allowed access outdoors, however for a new cat she should be kept indoors for at least three to four weeks to familiarise herself with the indoor environment, and should be neutered prior to being allowed to explore outside.

It is not just horizontal space that needs to be considered, vertical space holds a much higher level of importance to our felines. Access to elevated surfaces or equipment can improve a sense of security and wellbeing, improving the overall welfare of cats in our homes. The elevated space could be the provision of secure ledges or high cat trees, but it doesn't need to be specially bought

A cat wall with multiple perches and climbing facilities, or a tall cat tree, provide lots of vertical space, and include scratching posts, play and rest areas.

equipment, it could just be high-up accessible spaces that the cat can safely access, such as shelving, bookcases or window seats.

Resources

One of the reasons behind the most common perceived feline behaviour problems is to do with resources, their availability (or lack of) and location. Cats can be notoriously 'picky' when it comes to their resources, and owners are not always aware of the impact resource choice, quantity and location, has on the cat's welfare. This lack of awareness also extends to serial cat owners or owners of multiple cats, as there may be a lack of appreciation regarding the individual needs of different cats.

Figure 1.2 provides a summary of some of the requirements and options regarding the different resources you can provide, and how you can enhance the use of the space to avoid conflict.

The consensus is that all cats should be provided with one litter tray per cat in the home, plus one additional litter tray, located in accessible spaces in the home. This applies whether cats have access to the outdoors or not, especially where access is restricted, or for when they choose not to go outside. This availability provides cats with a choice of where to toilet, and a clean alternative should one tray have already been used. Cleanliness is also important to cats, and many won't use soiled trays, so ensuring trays are cleaned regularly is an important part of their welfare upkeep. Avoid strongly scented cleaners, and choose pet friendly, low odour options, used sparingly. Trays should be disinfected when necessary and then rinsed and dried to prevent disinfectant residue and potential ingestion. Some cats also prefer some of their own scent left behind; this is especially true for young kittens who are toilet training. Leaving a small amount of wet litter encourages re-use of the area and can prevent inappropriate elimination elsewhere in the home.

The type of tray and substrate are open to individual preferences. There are options for high sided or hooded trays, or the traditional shallow tray, which may be preferential

	Sleeping and resting	Toileting area	Eating	Enrichment
Locations	Locations that are high up such as ledges, as well as low down options. Sleeping locations outside or in sheds and garages to provide more options. Separate areas that are more isolated and chosen by the cat.	Provide latrine spaces ideally in multiple areas of the house. These should be placed in quiet locations away from the cats' feeding areas. If there is a location that the cat prefers it may be beneficial to place a latrine space there.	Locate water away from the feeding station. Make sure there is adequate distance between each individual's feeding station (this will be dependent on the individuals). Food and water bowls should be placed away from resting and toileting areas, and could be high up for more nervous individuals.	Vertical spaces to climb within the home, tall cat trees or ledges. Scent-marking places could be anywhere such as doorways, walking routes or resting places, and can be positioned horizontally or vertically. Outside spaces (enclosure, enclosed garden, free-roaming).
Types	Different types of exposure such as igloos to hide in or open beds that provide a view. Large sharing beds vs singular options. Existing locations such as sofas, beds or blankets.	Different types of trays such as hooded, high-lipped, corner trays, etc. Different types of substrates such as clumping, odourless, wooden pellets, etc.	Provision of wet and dry food options dependent on individual needs. Food enrichment using treat mats or treat balls. Cats should not be given dairy products such as cows' milk.	Things to scratch (scratch-posts and scratch mats) using preferential materials such as sisal rope, wood or cardboard. Make sure scratch posts are tall enough for the individual and have a heavy base. Have a variety of different types of toys such as things to chase (balls, feather toys, wands and dangling toys, etc), self-play toys, and many more. Things to encourage facial rubbing such as wall combs and brushes for grooming.
Number	No of cats +1	No of cats +1	Each cat should have a separate feeding station and there should be multiple water stations.	As many as possible, but these should continue to be rotated so that they remain novel and enriching.

Figure 1.2. Resource ideas for cats, including tips for when space within the home is limited.

Example layout of some of the resources required by a cat.

important to acknowledge which areas within the house are already favoured by your cat and then ensure resting at height is available to them in that area. There may be a reluctance to use a resting area if it is placed somewhere a cat deems as undesirable. Resting areas also need to be thought of in a similar manner to litter trays, in that multiple places should be offered, especially in multi-cat homes.

All these resources, along with the provision of enrichment, are important to improve a cat's welfare and avoid frustrations growing.

If the cat is new to the environment, then a mixture of her current resources, which will have a familiar scent, and some new resources should be included in the environment. New resources can be gradually added to the environment and the cat's confidence built around

to some. Litter substrate availability includes paper, wood, gravel and clay, but some may even prefer less common types such as soil. Understanding the preferences of your cats is an important step in creating appropriate resources in a welfare-friendly space. Each individual cat should have access to her own feed and water stations, which are also away from litter trays. Cats do not like to eat where they toilet, so clean and separate feeding and toileting areas, independent of another cats' resources, are paramount. The area should also be quiet and calm, in a non-social area where possible.

Felines tend to favour height when it comes to resting areas and therefore multiple off-the-ground sleeping areas should be offered. This helps to reduce any potential conflict, not only between cats, but also with dogs and children. Having obvious areas of perceived safety can support wellbeing as well as maintaining positive relationships. It is

the resources where necessary, as described in Chapter 2, so as not to overwhelm her; this is particularly relevant for less adaptable or resilient cats. Introducing their familiar odour to the environment is likely to reduce their stress; for example, placing current used litter into a new litter tray.

The locations of these resources are also worth careful consideration from the beginning, as prior to introducing two cats it is important to keep them separate from each other during the early stages, to let each cat settle into her new environment, therefore creating a safe space with new resources for her, as described in the next chapter. It is useful to have additional resources placed around the house ensuring there are plenty of alternative options to access, particularly when you are first introducing cats to each other or a new environment. Where resources, such as litter trays, beds and scratch

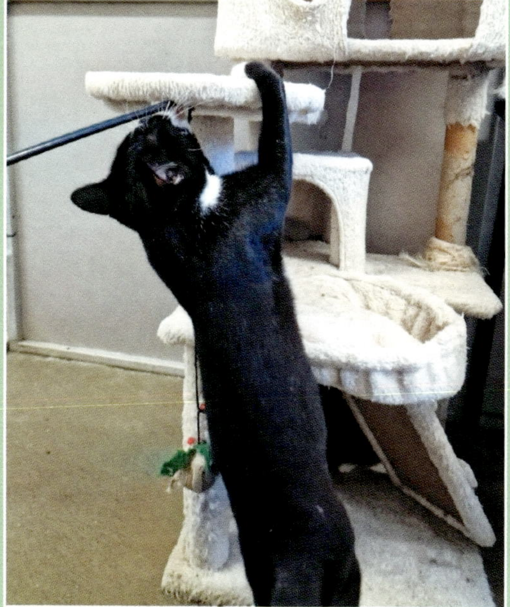

Using a toy to entice a cat to use a scratch post.

posts, are being added to an environment, these should be dispersed throughout the environment as much as possible.

Opportunities for scent marking are a priority for cats, and something that many caregivers do not consider. A significant portion of feline communication is all down to scent, and the ability to share that scent among resources within the house are key to more harmonious living. Scent marking also enables a cat to feel safe and secure in its environment. Access to scratching posts or cat trees in various areas of the home not only offers vertical space for cats to utilise as resting areas, but also to ensure they can leave their scent through scratching and rubbing. Cats have scent glands throughout their bodies, with facial glands around cheeks, chin and forehead, and in the paw pads, being commonly used on resources as well as caregivers (Figure 1.3).

Figure 1.3. The facial scent gland locations on a cat, highlighted in pink.

Cats will also scratch surfaces as part of scent marking and therefore scratch posts are a must to prevent cats scratching furniture and other undesired surfaces. You may also need to train young cats how to use new equipment and resources, such as entice them to go near and use the scratch post by using incentives. You can place food high up on the scratch post so that they have to stretch up the scratch the post to reach it, or encourage them by dangling a toy around it. To promote use of scratching equipment, try to position it in a desirable area, and not one which causes anxiety or frustration due to inappropriate location, for example in high traffic areas.

Some cats may have a stronger preference for horizontal scratching surfaces so the inclusion of coir matting or similar material, can replicate the use of a scratch post by still enabling scent marking. A mixture of both options can be provided and encouraged until a preference is identified. Make sure these areas are not washed regularly, especially with chemicals.

Remember that all cats are individual, and therefore where one area may be deemed desirable for one cat, it may not have the same appeal to another. The types of resources may also differ, so owners need to be particularly mindful in multi-cat households that they are meeting the needs of all cats, and not just some. Having a keen understanding of the types of cats within a household can make a significant positive difference to their welfare and reduce potential conflict between feline and caregiver, or other members of the household.

Restrictions

As briefly discussed, there are elements of our felines day-to-day life that impart some level of restriction. From their feeding schedule to having their freedom of movement restricted, or a feeling of restriction using collars. A perceived lack of control can lead to feelings of stress and frustration amongst individuals, which in turn will impact welfare negatively.

With any domestic animal, it is important to allow choice wherever it is possible and safe to do so. Cats can be provided with choice with regards to where they rest, eat and toilet, and the resources available to them. These choices may not seem like much, but they will support better wellbeing and reduce feelings of frustration that can occur. For some cats, the choice to go outdoors can also improve their wellbeing, and using a cat flap ensures free access when desired. This isn't a requirement of allowing outdoor access, however, as many cats 'tell' us when they want to leave or enter, or make use of a suitable window.

Multi-pet households

Multi-pet households are very common, with cats being one of the most popular pets. In the UK there are currently around 12.5 million cats, living in 29% of households, and based on the number of households within the UK, it can be estimated this equates to just over 8 million homes. Add to this the 13.5 million dogs, 1.5 million birds and 1 million rabbits, amongst other pets, currently living in our homes, we know many cats are living in a multi-pet household of some sort (PFMA, 2024). Multi-pet households come with their own benefits and challenges (Figure 1.4), and this book aims to consider some of the sociability factors that can affect how harmonious these environments can be.

As discussed within this first chapter, there are varied perceptions of cats, some based on historic views, and others much more recent. There are also many considerations that need to be taken into account when designing and maintaining a suitable home for our feline companions.

The remainder of the book will focus on three specific interactions between: cats and other cats, cats and dogs, and cats and children, as well as how to work on sociability and ensure more harmonious living between all involved.

Positive impacts	Negative impacts
Social interaction: Particularly social cats will benefit from positive social interactions with many different species as well as their own. **Improved wellbeing:** Individuals may engage in play behaviours, which increases overall activity levels and mental stimulation. **Reduced loneliness:** Positive interactions can reduce loneliness, especially if caregivers are out of the home for long periods.	**Competition for resources:** If adequate and suitable resources are not provided, there will be competition, which in turn leads to conflict and stress. **Conflict:** Personality can impact the amount and level of conflict that could arise in multi-pet households. Constant conflict or fear of threat can lead to chronic anxiety and stress. **Reduced attention:** A cat who seeks connection and contact with their caregivers may find the prospect of 'sharing' unappealing. **Stress:** The negative impacts can cause stress overall, specifically through cats existing in an anxious state due to other animals in the house.

Figure 1.4. The positive impacts (benefits) and negative impacts (challenges) of having a multi-pet household.

2: Cat communication

Cat behaviour is influenced by a variety of factors, including genetics and life experiences. We need to be able to interpret and understand our cat's behaviour so that we can provide the best possible welfare for that individual and prevent the development of potentially problematic behaviours. It is also helpful to have a good understanding about a cat's behaviour to be able to successfully integrate her into a family. This is particularly important when housing her with other cats, dogs and/or children. In this chapter we will be covering:

- The factors that influence a cat's behaviour
- How to interpret cat behaviour
- How to carry out a feline behaviour assessment, to measure cat sociability
- Some initial guidance on socialisation, managing arousal and creating safe spaces

First, however, we will introduce the FELID approach; this is the process we will follow like a checklist when introducing a cat to other cats, dogs, babies or children.

2.1 The FELID approach

The FELID approach is a guide that can be followed to establish and maintain safe and harmonious relationships between your cat and the rest of the family. This approach considers whether a cat can successfully live with other cats, dogs, babies and/or children, and how to encourage harmonious relationships within the household. The FELID approach includes five stages:

1. Assessing the individuals involved
2. Preparing the environment
3. Carrying out some training
4. Managing the first interactions
5. Monitoring the ongoing dynamics between the individuals (Figure 2.1)

This approach can be used to assess new family members to predict how likely they are to succeed in certain social situations, and it can also be used to improve current dynamics within a household.

The aim of this approach is to avoid anxiety or conflict between your cat and other members of the family, therefore improving the welfare of all individuals involved. This approach will be used as a guide throughout the next three chapters, and you should bear in mind that if the dynamics between individuals change, you'll need to reassess the situation, including reassessing the individuals and the environment to make the necessary modifications. Therefore, the FELID approach should be a continuous cycle of reflection that sets up your family to succeed.

2.2 Factors influencing behaviour

There are many factors that influence a cat's behaviour. Understanding some of these effects on behaviour can be useful for improving their welfare, including:

- Preventing the development of undesirable behaviours
- Avoiding causes of stress and reducing stress by adjusting our approaches and husbandry practices

FELINE FRIENDS	This stage includes assessing all individuals prior to introductions, to set them up for success. The assessments will include gaining an understanding about the individuals' behaviour, as well as about their previous experiences around cats, dogs, and people. Based on these assessments we will then make the necessary preparations ready for the introduction, which includes setting up the **environment**.
ENVIRONMENT	This stage is focused on setting up the environment for success prior to meeting. This will include adding resources and managing the space to meet the needs of the individuals; it will also include establishment of safe spaces. As part of this preparation it is also important to do some training, leading us to the next stage, **learning**.
LEARNING	This stage will include preparing the individuals for meeting, including scent sharing and building confidence in cats, particularly when they are in view of the other cats, dogs, babies and children. This stage also includes preparation training for dogs, and education for children. This should be done prior to physical **interactions**.
INTERACTIONS	This stage focuses on the first physical interactions between the individuals, and how to make these safe and positive. Continuous monitoring will then be required to manage all ongoing social **dynamics**.
DYNAMICS	This stage will focus on the ongoing monitoring and management of interactions, and the dynamics between individuals, including troubleshooting common problems. You should always monitor interactions, as many factors can modify behaviours in cats, dogs and children. Even in long-term relationships it is important to be aware of changes in individuals and their behaviour, so you should continue to assess your felines and their **feline friends**.

Figure 2.1. A description of the FELID approach.

- Reducing the instance of cats being relinquished
- Improving success when rescuing and rehoming cats

Behaviour is influenced by many factors, including the characteristics that a cat is born with (genetics), her lifetime experiences (emotional events and learning), and a cat's health (including physiological changes due to age and health), as seen in Figure 2.2. These factors are all interconnected and will alter a cat's overall perception and therefore how she will behave in various situations. For example, how a cat behaves around a dog would depend on her inborn traits (how bold she is), her lifetime experiences (if she has previously had positive experiences around dogs), and her overall health (if she is in pain). This section will focus on these three factors in further detail.

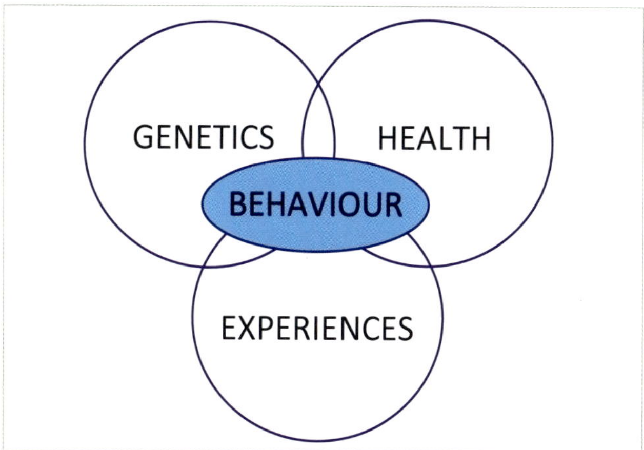

Figure 2.2. Three factors that influence the behaviour of cats. These are interrelated, as genetics and experiences can have an impact on physical and mental health; genetics and health will influence a cat's perception and therefore their experiences; and lifetime experiences and health can both have an influence on genes and how they are expressed.

Genetic influences on behaviour

Genetics will have an impact on an individual's external and internal characteristics. Understanding and predicting cat behaviour is based upon generalisations made using current knowledge of species-typical behavioural repertoires, such as when a cat may hiss when scared or during conflict. The domestic cat is largely unaltered in its morphological features and behavioural characteristics (vocalisations, postures and movements) from its ancestors. This allows us to make some inferences as to their emotional state and stress levels, which can be useful for maintaining a high level of welfare. It is also pertinent to always consider individual differences.

Over time the diversity of cat breeds has increased, which has led to some morphological and behavioural differences. Morphological features can have an impact on a cat's health but may also impact natural behavioural patterns such as being able to communicate. For example, cats that are lacking a tail will not be able to use their tail for visual communicative signals, such as gesturing their intentions. Breeds or breed types are also known to exhibit certain traits or behaviours, such as the active and curious nature of Bengal cats. Genetics will also play a role in determining how sociable a cat is, as it is the blueprint for their personality and behaviours. However, this is only part of what influences behaviour as throughout her lifetime a cat will have experiences that will influence her perception and therefore influence her future behaviour. For example, a cat that has been raised around dogs, and has had a lot of previous positive relationships with dogs, is more likely to be successful when being housed with a dog in a family.

Lifetime experiences

In addition to the variety of innate (species-specific) behaviours that will influence how a cat may behave, she will also learn from experiences throughout her life that will adjust her behaviour to be very individual. Experiences are any events or occurrences that can leave an impression on a cat, such as social experiences, which include encounters with other individuals in the environment. All experiences throughout a cat's life will have an influence on behaviour; however, the level of influence will depend on a range of factors, including:

- The individual's personality
- Other environmental factors including the presence of other animals and how they behave
- The type or intensity of the event
- Previous learning and the success of previous behavioural strategies
- The cat's current health
- The cat's emotional state

In this section we will focus on learning theory and emotional states, as these are essential to consider when introducing cats to new individuals and when promoting positive emotional states and desired behaviour.

Learning happens throughout a cat's lifetime; however, early experiences can have a massive impact on cat behaviour. There is a sensitive period in which kittens are highly responsive to the formation of social bonds. The timing of this period is genetically determined and is around two to seven weeks of age. During this period a kitten may develop their food preferences, litter substrate preferences, and avoidance behaviours. After this period, a fear reaction becomes fully established and it is therefore best to encourage positive experiences around novelty before seven weeks of age, which can be done through socialisation.

Socialisation is the process where a cat will learn how to recognise, interact, and bond with other species that she lives with, as well as learn to accept novel experiences and events. During socialisation it is important for her to have positive exposures to other cats, other animals, people, and a variety of stimuli (anything that can trigger a response) in the environment; this is a key factor in the prevention of fear. Every interaction provides a learning opportunity and will have an impact on her perception and behaviour, and because of effective socialisation she can be friendlier, more confident, and could have fewer problems with aggression. However, be aware that cats will typically be more cautious of unfamiliar cats than with those they know, regardless of how well-socialised they are, and therefore introductions to new individuals will always need to be structured. These interactions will all modify her perception and therefore her behaviour.

Learning can occur in a variety of ways including through observational learning and associative learning. Observational learning is when kittens observe the behaviour of others, for example if a mother cat demonstrates a fear response towards people, then her kittens are likely to also show this behaviour, and it can then be more difficult to reverse this learning after the sensitive period. Associative learning is when a cat learns from her own experiences, by learning about connections between two or more stimuli (respondent conditioning) or from consequences of her own behaviour (operant conditioning). These are approaches often used when training cats to modify perceptions, encourage desired behaviour, and improve the chance of success when introducing cats to other members of the family (Figure 2.3).

Respondent conditioning is purely the presentation of a novel stimuli alongside a stimulus that already triggers a specific behaviour or emotional state, and, after repeated presentations together, the novel stimuli will lead to the same behaviour or emotional state. For example, by presenting desirable food treats every time your cat is in the presence of a child then they are more likely to build a positive emotional state around the child. So, for respondent conditioning the behaviour or emotional state is the indirect outcome of the association, whereas for operant conditioning the behaviour is what is being directly encouraged or discouraged.

When behaviour leads to a satisfactory state (avoids something unpleasant or receives something pleasant) then the future likelihood of that behaviour being performed again increases, whereas if a behaviour leads to an unsatisfactory state (receives something unpleasant or loses something pleasant) then the future likelihood of that behaviour decreases. Behaviours can be internally reinforced, for example if a cat avoids people and stays safe then she is likely to avoid people again in the future, or externally reinforced, for example if the same cat approaches people and gets a food treat then she is likely to approach people again.

We often actively encourage a desirable behaviour by presenting something she perceives as pleasant such as food treats; this is known as positive reinforcement. However, desirable behaviours can also be reinforced when something she perceives as undesirable is taken away; that is known as negative reinforcement. For example, if she stays calm and relaxed in the dog's presence while we move the dog's attention away from her then this will increase the likelihood of her calm behaviour in the dog's presence in future, while also possibly improving her confidence in the dog's presence.

Over time, practised responses can become habits or part of a cat's typical behavioural patterns; however,

Learning theory	What the cat learns	How it can be used in practice
Respondent conditioning	The cat builds an association between two stimuli or events.	This method is used to build confidence in cats by providing desirable food around novel stimuli, novel environments, or during interactions (eg brushing). It can be used to teach a recall by pairing a recall cue (eg the cat's name) with a desirable reward (eg attention or food treat).
Operant conditioning	The cat builds an association between a behaviour and its consequence.	This can be used to encourage a desired behaviour by providing something pleasant (a reinforcer) to the cat, such as food, attention.

Figure 2.3. Overview of respondent and operant conditioning and how they can be used in practice when training cats.

Emotional state	Motivational triggers	Behavioural indicators of the emotions
Investigatory and seeking	• Seeking resources such as food, space, or novel stimuli, or interaction with the environment.	• Approaching stimuli and being inquisitive. • Environmental investigation such as searching and sniffing. • Playing with toys or the environment. • Hunting behaviours, such as crouching and ambush behaviours.
Lust	• Sexual desire usually from the presence of the opposite sex.	• Searching or pacing, particularly in the presence of a cat of the opposite sex. • Vocalisations such as yeowling. • Increased scent marking such as spraying.
Care	• Caring for another individual, such as offspring.	• Rubbing up alongside the other individual. • Allogrooming (grooming other individuals)
Joyous	• Play and social interaction	• Play behaviours with a conspecific or other animal (chasing, jumping, biting, hiding).
Fear or anxiety	• Startled or scared of a stimulus or anything where they are avoiding an interaction or attempting to increase distance between themselves and a stimulus.	• Avoidance, hiding, fleeing, escape behaviours. • Aggressive responses (hissing, spitting, scratching).
Frustration	• A result of escape (fear) being thwarted. • Resources not being accessible, such as food, space, or not being able to get to another individual (eg, a sexual mate, an attachment figure, or a rival). • Over-arousal or frustration driven by lust. • Over-arousal during play. • Defence of self or of offspring.	• Increased scent-making, destructive behaviours, vocalisations such as yowling, and aggressive responses, such as redirected aggression.
Attachment distress	• Lonely and sad from being without an attachment figure or other social individual.	• Searching for the other individual (restlessness). • Vocalisations such as short meows.

Figure 2.4. Some of the emotional states that influence behaviours in cats, along with possible motivational triggers and behavioural indicators of the emotional states.

emotional state is also an important factor that influences a cat's behaviour and learning. Emotional states can be negative or positive and are likely to lead to specific behaviour patterns, as demonstrated in Figure 2.4, although this will vary from individual to individual based on prior learning and what has previously worked for them. For example, even though two cats may both be fearful of other cats and want to increase space between themselves and another cat, one might avoid and hide whereas the other might approach offensively to get the other cat to move away. Behaviours can therefore be self-reinforcing, for example if a cat shows avoidance behaviour and stays safe then she is likely to show avoidance in a similar situation or in the presence of the same stimulus.

Health influences on behaviour

Health can influence behaviour in many ways, and may also have an impact on how a cat perceives situations. If a cat is in pain, she may be more irritable or be more reactive in stressful situations. Therefore, prior to introductions, make sure that she is free of discomfort or pain. Behaviour and health will also alter as a cat gets older, therefore it's worth considering age prior to introductions. Older cats who have had a lot of positive experiences around a range of animals and people, or kittens who are more flexible in their learning (particularly before seven weeks of age), will be the easiest cats to introduce to new members of the family. As a cat gets older, they may go through cognitive deterioration or health changes that could increase the likelihood of pain; this may change how they interact with new or current members of the family, so continuous monitoring of behavioural changes is important.

It is best to avoid introducing new members to the family if you have a cat that is pregnant, has kittens, is reaching sexual maturity, has a chronic or acute health condition, has experienced a stressful event such as a house move, has recently been rehomed, or is currently in a stressful environment. If this can't be avoided then extra care should be taken during the introductions, usually progressing through the stages at a slower rate and keeping the individuals in separate spaces for a longer period of time.

A cat's physiological state will also influence behaviour; for example when a cat is hungry or tired she is more likely to be irritable, restless, or redirect her frustration onto nearby individuals. Therefore, it's important to manage resources and provide relevant behavioural outlets. We discussed the importance of resources in Chapter 1, and will refer to these more specifically throughout the next three chapters regarding managing and supporting interactions.

2.3 Interpreting cat behaviour

Being able to read and interpret body language and communicative signals of cats is essential when it comes to understanding your cat's emotional state, avoiding being scratched or bitten and maintaining harmony within the family. Communication allows cats to exchange information with other individuals, so that they can avoid conflict and communicate their intentions. This is important to bear in mind when assessing your cat prior to introductions, but also during any interactions she has.

This section covers general communication signals of cats, including general behaviour patterns and arousal. Some of a cat's responses and patterns of behaviour are instinctive and are driven by biologically relevant stimuli, such as when protecting young, whereas others are dependent on her experiences over time.

When reading and interpreting a cat's behaviour, consider the following:

Reading behaviour

1. All body postures and movements; for example, her tail movements as well as her body position and vocalisations, rather than just one element of her behaviour such as specifically focusing on her tail movements.
2. The types of vocalisations, duration and pitch.
3. The direction and orientation of the behaviour (approach vs avoidance) and how she is shifting her weight (shifting towards or away).

Interpreting behaviour

1. The context of the situation and, where possible, the causes.
2. Understanding the individual's normal behaviour as well as typical species-specific and/or breed-specific behaviour.

For the most part we will focus on the typical species-specific behaviours for cats, however, make sure you consider the situation and what maybe unique for the individual when interpreting responses. You should also acknowledge that some breeds of cats might differ in their likelihood to perform behaviours, their speed at responding, and/or their ability to communicate certain signals or postures. This can be dependent on their morphology or temperament, and can make interactions more challenging for these breeds. For example, Bengal cats are often more intense in their behaviours, which could make other cats more nervous, and brachycephalic breeds, such as Persians, have more limited facial expressions compared to other breeds, which is likely to limit their ability to communicate effectively.

We know that cats exchange information frequently and effectively via scent in the form of pheromonal distribution. Scent marking is when a cat distributes chemical signals into the environment. There are several behaviours that are indicative of scent marking including scratching, facial rubbing and urine marking. The distribution of scent can be a big factor in avoiding conflict, maintaining cohesion and building bonds between cats within social groups. Cats will rub their cheeks against furniture and people to distribute their scent, but will also rub against other familiar cats to create a shared scent, or scratch surfaces to distribute scent on items within their territory. Urine marking is another form of scent distribution, but can also be seen when a cat becomes fearful or frustrated and/or if there isn't the opportunity to practice facial rubbing or scratching. Where possible, facial rubbing and scratching should be encouraged by providing the necessary resources, such as scratch posts, as described in Chapter 1.

Positive emotional state (Relaxed)	**Negative emotional state (Stressed)**
Body: relaxed body postures during movements and possibly laid on their stomach, side or on their back. Slow ventilation.	Body: spine or back may be arched or the cat may be crouched low to the ground on top of all fours, shaking. The stomach will not be exposed and legs are likely to be tucked under the body as a protective and adaptive posture to move quickly if required and to protect themselves. Movements could be slow and tense with fast ventilation.
Eyes: normal pupils, with closed or half opened eyes.	Eyes: fully opened eyes and dilated pupils.
Ears: ears would be half-back or normal for the individual. They could be erected when alert.	Ears: are likely to be fully flattened or partially flattened ears, put to the sides or back against the head.
Tail: the tail could be extended or loosely wrapped. It may be twitching or moving gently and may have a soft curve.	Tail: the tail will be close to the body, such as being tucked in or curled forward around the body or could be arched and puffed up if part of an agonistic or fearful response. It could be moving in a forceful way and possibly thumping it against the ground.
Head: would be laid on surface or above the body if stood, chin up or on a surface, maybe some movement. Whiskers are likely lateral to be forward.	Head: the head is likely to be motionless and lower than the body. Mouth may be open, panting, or the cat could be spitting. Whiskers are likely to be back.
Vocalisations: the cat could be vocalising in specific contexts such as to gain attention or food including chirrups or meows, or there could be no vocalisations.	Vocalisations: may have a sorrowful meow, yowling, growling or hissing. Alternatively there may be minimal vocalisations due to fear.
Activities: activities would be typical for the individual such as sleeping or resting, exploring or playing.	Activities: activities will be focused around trying to escape or cat will be motionless.

Figure 2.5. Behavioural indicators of negative and positive emotional states in cats.

A cat approaching as part of a greeting response with the tail held upright, ears forward and erect, and moving forward with loose, relaxed movements.

The images above show cats relaxed and resting. Their behaviour is indicative of relaxed cats that are in a positive emotional state, holding whiskers to the side, body stretched out with the stomach either semi or fully exposed.

The lower two images are more indicative of a cat in a negative emotional state. The ears are swivelled sideways, the body is hunched and tense, the eyes are open with wide pupils and the tail is tucked around the body. When cats are particularly scared then they may arch their back, and fluff up the fur on their back and tail.

Behaviour patterns

Behaviour is driven by emotional states, as identified in Figure 2.4, and certain behaviour patterns can be indicative of these emotional states. A cat who is relaxed or in a positive emotional state will tend to perform behaviours that are part of her typical daily activities, such as grooming and sleeping, but is also likely to exhibit inquisitive and playful behaviour. Her movements will generally be more relaxed, and she may perform kneading, which is a behaviour that a cat performs when at ease. Kneading is when a cat pushes her front paws alternately against a surface accompanied by a grasping motion of the claws. A cat may also flex her paws in the

	RED	AMBER	GREEN
RESILIENCE	Startle response possibly followed by avoidance and hiding, and takes a long time to recover.	Startle response may be seen but recovers well.	Startle response may be seen but easily distracted and recovers quickly.
	May show undesirable behaviours and/or signs of fear or frustration, such as extreme avoidance and hiding, urine spraying, scratching or aggressive responses.	May show some signs of fear or frustration but these are minor in the form of avoidance or possible vocalisations such as hissing.	May be minor discomfort after the startle response but it is not long lasting and does not lead to additional undesirable behaviours.
CONFIDENCE	Very flighty and is likely to flee. Does not take treats or actively avoids treats/attention.	May stay in one location and stare or sniff from a distance. May take treats or accept attention in the presence of the stimuli but maintains caution.	Willing to approach and sniff, take treats and seek attention in the presence of novel stimuli.
	Fearful and avoidant behaviours observed (crouched or tucked body posture, ears back, tension around the face, slow and stiff movements, and stiff tail and under body).	Some caution seen with potentially minor fearful behaviours observed (avoiding, looking/ turning away, low ears, some tension around the face).	Relaxed body language (soft, relaxed body posture, relaxed low-set ears, tail low, no tension around the face, loose, floppy movements).
	Does not engage in a large range of additional behaviours such as playing.	May engage in additional behaviours such as cautious investigation.	Will engage in a range of behaviours, such as play behaviours, investigatory behaviours, grooming, scratching, eating, sleeping.
ADAPTABLE	Struggles with change, even the most minor changes to the environment.	Does not struggle too much with change.	Does not struggle at all with change.
	Does not adapt to the environment or changes and may show signs of chronic or acute stress.	Adapts to the changes but shows caution and possibly some minor stress.	Adapts to the changes well and either has not noticed or shows any care, or increases investigatory behaviours and facial rubbing.

Figure 2.6. RAG (red, amber, green) rating of how you can understand your cat's resilience, confidence and adaptability. Every cat will, of course, behave with a different level of these traits dependent on the context and situation.

air in a kneading motion while laid down. This behaviour goes back to kittenhood where the behaviour would be performed to stimulate milk production through the release of oxytocin. It is likely retained into adulthood as a method of communication with humans to signal affiliation and is often reinforced with affection and attention.

Cats that are stressed or in a negative emotional state will be more likely to hide, be more unpredictable in their responses, groom more than usual and not continue with their typical daily activities. The movements of cats in a negative emotional state can be slow, particularly during agonistic interactions, which are social interactions involving conflict. Even though vocalisations are unique to an individual, generally during negative emotional states vocalisations tend to be higher pitched and will include yowls and growls. Whereas vocalisations during positive emotional states are generally more pleasant, and can include chirrups and meows, as highlighted in Figure 2.5 along with some other typical indicators of a cat in a positive or negative emotional state.

A cat who is very confident, resilient and adaptable is more likely to be able to adjust to living with other cats, dogs and children successfully. A confident cat is more relaxed, engages in typical behaviours such as play, and is more likely to investigate environments and be friendly. Resilience is the ability to withstand or recover quickly, ie, bounce back, from difficulties or scary situations, and therefore going back quickly to the individual's typical behaviour. Adaptability is the ability to adjust to changes in the environment; be aware, however, that just because a cat may be resilient, confident or adaptable in one situation it does not mean that they will be in all situations. It can therefore be helpful to gauge these traits in your cat (Figure 2.6) and be aware of how your cat may react to change.

Agonistic interactions are often driven by negative emotions, and include aggressive displays, warning signals, appeasement signals, and avoidance behaviours. These behaviours will usually occur between unfamiliar individuals, but can also occur between familiar individuals in situations that cause fear or frustration, such as not being able to access resources or space, which can cause an individual to redirect their frustration onto others. Play behaviours can include similar behaviours such as chasing, swiping at each other, biting each other and pouncing on each other; however, there are differences.

True agonistic interactions are ritualised, and often begin a lot slower than playful behaviour patterns. During these interactions' cats are likely to have piloerection (erect fur across body and fluffed up tail), an arched back or tense body, ears back, intense staring, they may have a sideways-on stance to display their size and are more likely to vocalise, for instance with a low-pitched growling. As arousal increases there may be more intense tail flicks and long unpleasant yowls, particularly before pouncing or chasing occurs. These behaviours are all indicators of displeasure and act as a deterrent to not come closer. They are used to increase distance between the individuals as a protective measure.

Playful behaviours on the other hand will usually present as cats having their ears forward and soft body movements that are more relaxed. They may also involve ambush-like behaviours such as stalking and bottom wiggling prior to pouncing. Not all individuals may be actively involved in the play, however, so it is important to make sure that it is reciprocal and not one-sided. If an interaction seems very one-sided, with one individual doing most of the pouncing and chasing while the other individual is showing more defensive or avoidance behaviours, such as being more vocal (hissing and growling), ears back, becoming still and staring, then they probably want the interaction to cease, so this is more indicative of an agonistic interaction.

Frustration can arise from play and therefore become an agonistic interaction, particularly when play is inappropriate. Inappropriate play can be when one cat constantly bothers another, or ignores the other cat's signals that they do not want to play. Frustration in cats can be subtle and difficult to detect, and may result in multiple behaviours such as redirected aggression, scratching, and urine spraying.

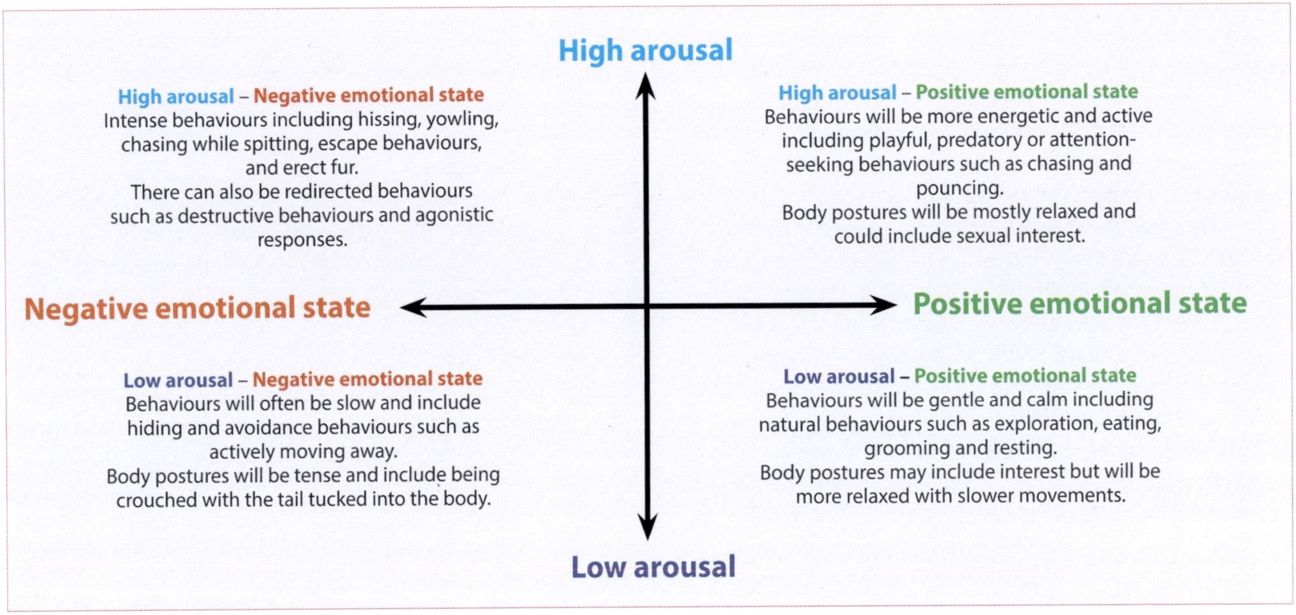

High arousal
High arousal – Negative emotional state
Intense behaviours including hissing, yowling, chasing while spitting, escape behaviours, and erect fur.
There can also be redirected behaviours such as destructive behaviours and agonistic responses.
High arousal – Positive emotional state
Behaviours will be more energetic and active including playful, predatory or attention-seeking behaviours such as chasing and pouncing.
Body postures will be mostly relaxed and could include sexual interest.
Negative emotional state
Positive emotional state
Low arousal – Negative emotional state
Behaviours will often be slow and include hiding and avoidance behaviours such as actively moving away.
Body postures will be tense and include being crouched with the tail tucked into the body.
Low arousal – Positive emotional state
Behaviours will be gentle and calm including natural behaviours such as exploration, eating, grooming and resting.
Body postures may include interest but will be more relaxed with slower movements.
Low arousal

Figure 2.7. Behaviours that are likely to be seen in cats during high and low arousal when in a positive and negative emotional state.

Aggressive behaviours either towards the cause of frustration or redirected towards something else. If the frustration occurs during an interaction there may be increased biting and fur flying or chase behaviours.
Redirected destruction such as scratching furniture, biting objects, knocking things over, or possible urine marking.
Fixation on a goal, increased vocalisations (meows, yowls, growls and hisses), increased persistence, or appearing more frantic.
Increased tail twitching, ears flattened, impatient pacing and more intense swatting during an interaction.
Calm and relaxed.

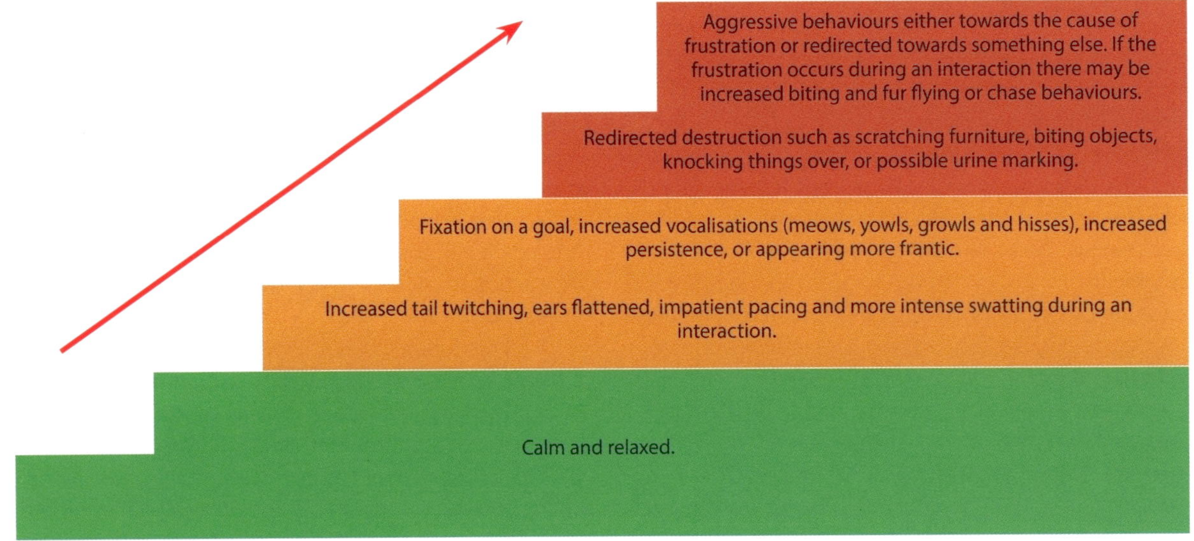

Figure 2.8. Increased arousal driven by frustration will increase the intensity of the behaviours as well as the types of behaviour seen.

Arousal in cats

Arousal is the state of being energised, excited or alert. Levels of arousal vary greatly and are usually linked to the physiological and emotional state of the individual, often resulting in more intense behaviours, higher likelihood of response, or more varied responses. Cats can be aroused by positive effects driven by excitement, a desire to play, and sexual desire, or by negative effects that make them want to protect themselves, usually driven by fear or frustration. Some of the signs and behaviours that may be seen during high and low arousal for both positive and negative emotional states are identified in Figure 2.7. However, be aware that specific behaviours will be unique to that individual. Some behaviours and interactions can naturally increase arousal, and, if a cat is highly aroused, their responses can become more intense through increased excitement or can lead to undesirable interactions.

Arousal can be difficult to distinguish in cats, particularly during interactions, as cats can seem calm and relaxed one minute and then dramatically change behaviour quickly during an interaction, including swiping out, grabbing arms, scratching or biting. These can be learnt interactions, and may be due to growing arousal from a negative effect, such as through frustration. This can be due to the type of interaction and as a way of ceasing or changing the interaction, or they can be from a positive effect, such as part of a play response, excitement during an interaction, or to engage in an interaction. It can also just

	A cat that becomes fearful or frustrated during interactions.	**A cat that gets over excited during interactions.**
Prevention	Avoid situations that your cat is scared of, or that trigger frustration. Avoid handling or touching your cat when she is in a negative emotional state or that may cause frustration.	Avoid playing with the cat with your hands, instead use extended toys. Avoid stroking head to tip of tail, instead stroke the cat where they enjoy with small strokes. Provide a range of enrichment and resources in the form of scratch posts and toys.
Management	Cease all interaction and move away. Provide the cat with some space, such as access outside or onto a vertical space. Provide enrichment as a distraction that changes the cat's emotional state, such as food or toys (particularly if frustration driven). Provide a range of resources in a range of locations so the cat is always able to access them, especially in multi-cat households where a cat is easily frustrated. Encourage your cat into their safe space (particularly if fear driven).	Cease any interaction and move away. Provide the cat with some space, such as access outside or onto a vertical space. If necessary you can redirect their excitement onto a toy or distract them with a toy or treats.

Figure 2.9. This table provides some tips on how to prevent high arousal occurring and how to manage high arousal that may become problematic during interactions.

be a learnt repertoire of how they interact with other cats, dogs or humans.

Some cats can become aroused very quickly with very few indicators beforehand, whereas other cats may demonstrate a lot of indicators as their arousal increases. If she is feeling fearful or frustrated, or even sexually aroused, then the arousal will develop in response to a specific resource or stimuli. If she is becoming excited or playful then it may be in response to a specific stimulus, or it could be a more generalised arousal where she might begin racing around the room in response to a range of stimuli. High arousal driven by fear is likely to present itself as either desperation to escape, or aggressive behaviours with defensive postures, whereas for high arousal driven by frustration the cat is more likely to display more direct aggressive behaviours and/or redirected aggression (Figure 2.8). Undesirable behaviours are usually linked to an increase in arousal, however even when cats are not demonstrating these behaviours and are in a state of low arousal, it does not mean that they are in a positive emotional state, and therefore their welfare is still affected, such as a cat becoming depressed, hiding or showing avoidance.

Managing arousal is important, both when introducing individuals and during interactions where you want to avoid agonistic interactions, or the cat getting too excited and playful and scratching or biting you. Arousal can be prevented and managed in multiple ways (Figure 2.9). Where possible it is important to avoid situations that may trigger an increase in arousal, but also to manage high arousal such as by using distraction or adjusting how you respond to her.

For cats that are more difficult to read, become quickly aroused, or if they are less sociable, it is important to avoid interactions that may trigger them. Altering how you interact with her is important; you could try playing with extendable toys that provide distance between her and your hand, or providing only short strokes in one location of the body. You should make sure that these interactions are pleasurable for her, as not all cats will want to engage in being touched, and will have their own preferences as to where on their body they like to be stroked. To prevent increased arousal, it can be useful to avoid stroking continuously down the length of the cat's body from head to tip of tail and avoid areas that may be sensitive, such as her stomach, feet or the tip of her tail. You should also stop stroking her during an interaction to allow her the opportunity to tell you whether she wants to continue or not, by either moving towards you, meowing at you, or looking at you. If she doesn't then it may be an indication that she is also happy to disengage. Conflict often arises between humans and cats when they are not provided with the opportunity to communicate their need to disengage from an interaction, often resulting in a swipe or bite. Offering her the time and space for this signal is important in managing arousal and reinforcing positive experiences.

2.4 Predicting feline sociability

Before introducing a cat to new members of the family, regardless of whether it is a new cat coming into a household or a current cat having a new member join the family (cat, dog or baby/child), it is important to assess her general behaviour and experiences to predict how likely she is to integrate successfully and live harmoniously with the new family member/s. The first key thing to check is her health, as if she is not well or in pain it will have a negative impact on introductions. Once she has been health-checked you should begin the relevant feline assessment to assess her potential sociability. If the cat is a true feral under two months old or a non-feral under four months old, then your cat is instantly scored as green. If she is a feral older than two months old or a non-feral over four months old, then you should complete one of the following assessments.

Feline assessments

As previously discussed, there are a range of factors that influence how a cat will respond in a situation, including her prior experiences. The person who spends most time with the cat or the caregiver should complete the assessment. The assessment consists of questions and statements on the cat's previous social experiences with other cats, dogs or children, and her overall behavioural tendencies and personality traits, based on her responses in everyday situations and to changes in the environment. The person completing the assessment should gauge her overall confidence and adaptability using the information from section 2.3 about interpreting cat behaviour. If the cat tolerates the other cat, dog or child then she would mostly just ignore their presence, not want to interact with them and/or prefer a certain distance from them. On the other hand, a flighty cat would be a cat that is easily startled, skittish and is likely to run away in the presence of a perceived stressor or threat.

If the question or statement applies to the cat in some situations but not others, please make a judgement as to how much you agree or disagree in the provision of your answer. Complete them all as best as you can but if you are unsure about any of the answers, or if her prior experiences are unknown, then just answer either *'No'* or *'Agree'*. If you are planning on introducing her to another cat use Feline Assessment 1 (Figure 2.10), if she is being introduced to a dog use Feline Assessment 2 (Figure 2.11), and if she is being introduced to a child, use Feline Assessment 3 (Figure 2.12).

The feline sociability predictor (FSP)

Using the result from the feline assessment/s that you have completed, you can now predict the likelihood of success the cat will have when being introduced to the new individual/s.

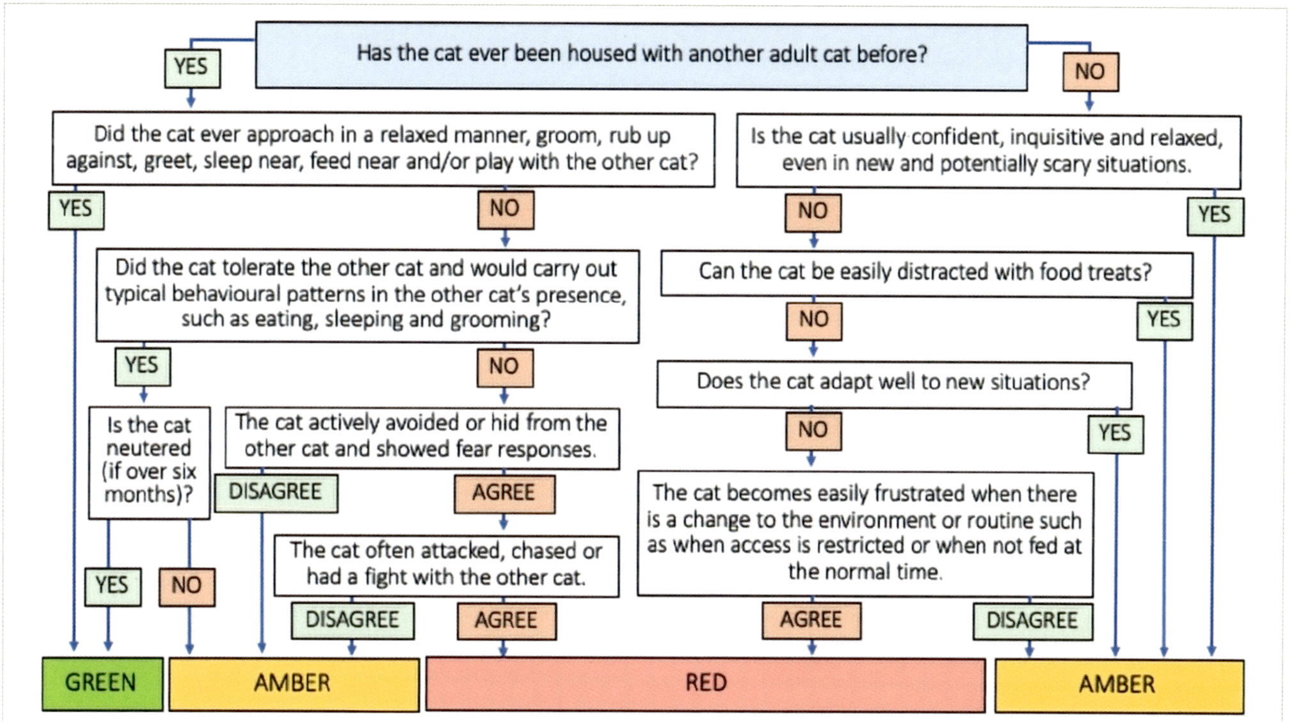

Figure 2.10. Feline Assessment 1: this assesses the cat's potential suitability to live with other adult cats. If you are unsure on any of the answers, then just choose 'No' or 'Agree'.

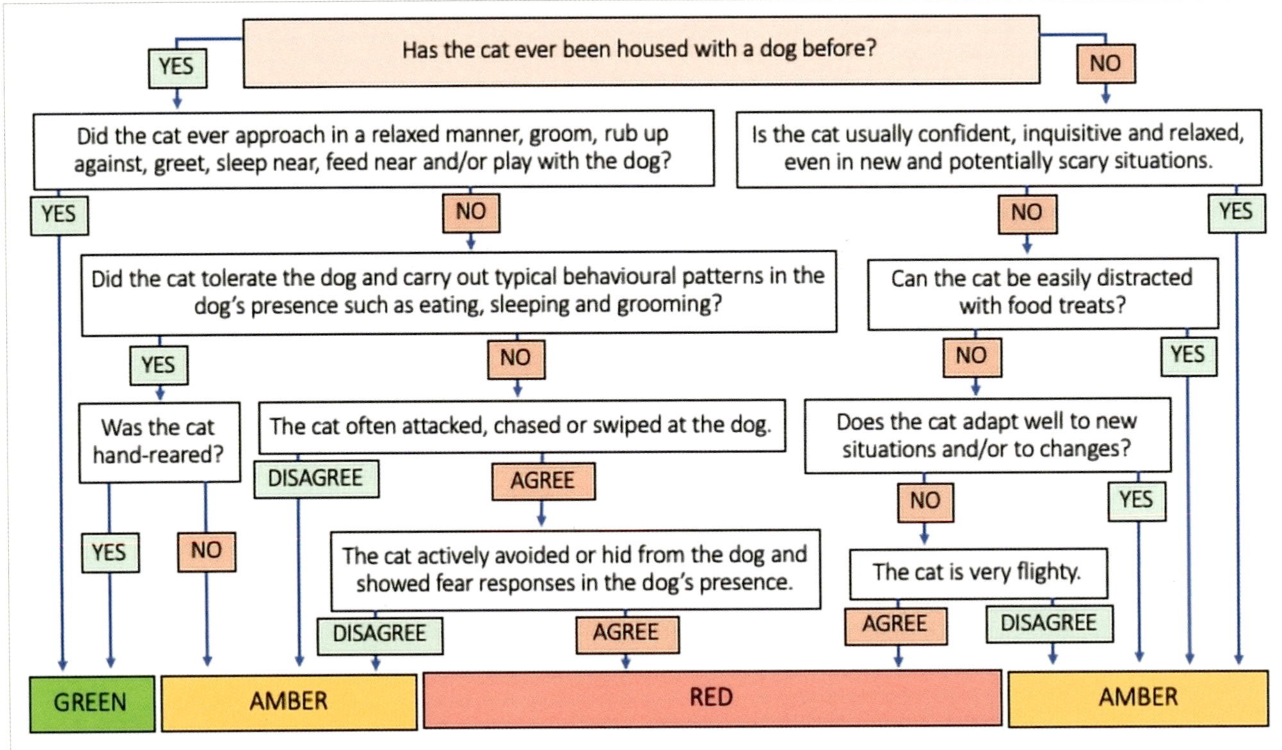

Figure 2.11. Feline Assessment 2: this assesses the cat's potential suitability to live with dogs. If you are unsure on any of the answers, then just choose 'No' or 'Agree'.

Green-rated cats are going to be the most likely to succeed when being introduced to a new individual, whereas those in the red category are less likely to be successful; amber category cats may be fine, but might need some additional time and space to undertake relevant training.

Remember, however, that the FSP score is based upon whether you are planning on introducing her to another cat, a dog or child, and a separate assessment may be required for other introductions. When introducing her to another cat, it is important to assess the other cat in the same way, and then follow the steps as described in Chapter 3, based on both cats' results. When introducing to a dog, he should also be assessed as described in Chapter 4, and when introducing to a child, it is important to educate the child prior to the introduction, as described in Chapter 5.

If you needed to complete multiple assessments (Feline Assessments 1, 2 and/or 3) on your cat, due to her being introduced to multiple species (cat, dog and/or child) then you may have come out with two or three different FSP results. Therefore, you should use the relevant chapters to improve the chances of having a successful introduction for each individual. Prior to introductions you should make sure that each cat is litter trained, have done some confidence building, and you have set up a safe space, guidance for which is discussed in the next section (2.5 Training).

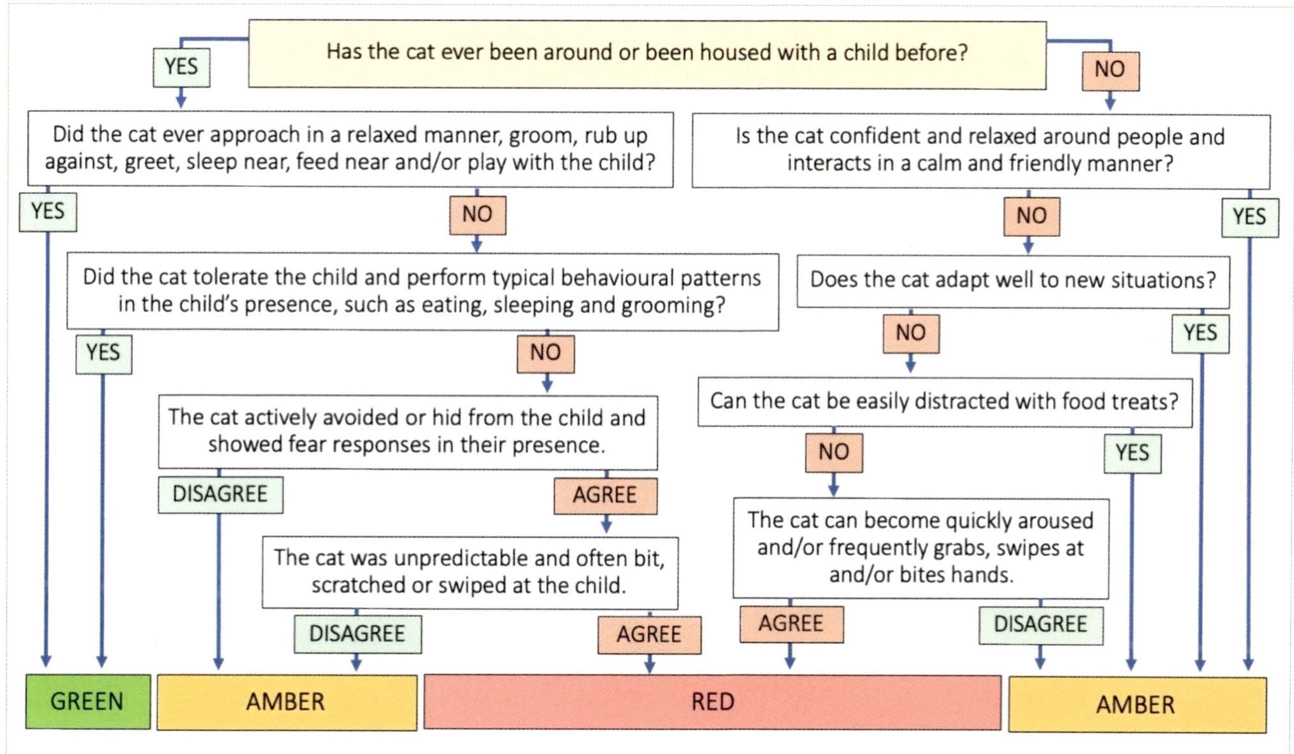

Figure 2.12. Feline Assessment 3: this assesses the cat's potential suitability to live with children. Where it states child, it also refers to multiple children, so give your answer considering all children the cat has interacted with or been around. If she has not lived with children before but has had experience of them visiting her home, you can complete the assessment based on her behaviour in that situation. If you are unsure on any of the answers, then just choose 'No' or 'Agree'.

2.5 Training

When cats are young it is important to socialise them to a range of situations, as it can build overall confidence and resilience. It is also important that kittens and young cats are housed, where possible, with other kittens or sociable cats. We should continue to build a cat's confidence, even as she gets older, as it will help her settle into new environments and adapt to change. There are a few things that can be done to modify her perception and behaviour, such as creating a safe space for her, and doing confidence-building exercises. By doing these it can help her feel more relaxed and allow her to adapt better to changes, such as integrating into a new family or accepting new members of the family.

Hand-reared kittens may lack feline social skills and may be hyperactive in object and social play. However, if a kitten can be housed with other cats in the home and engaged in play sessions with wand-type toys, this may provide them with key skills.

Prior to undertaking training, it is important to make a list of any pleasant stimuli that you can use during training to modify her perceptions and behaviour. Food is naturally reinforcing, and if a cat eats in an environment, in the presence of a range of stimuli, it can help her build her confidence in that situation. Try a range of food treats with your cat to gauge her interest, and find out which are her favourites (higher-value treats), you can also gauge whether she finds verbal praise or touch pleasurable, as these may also be useful as possible emotional or behavioural reinforcers. This can be done by simply preference testing a range of food and toy items, as well as different forms of human interaction, and seeing which she chooses to spend more time exploring or engaging with. Once these are compared with each other, for example, wand toys, mouse toys, mobile toys etc, the most popular can then be compared with the most popular from other categories, to determine which is the most reinforcing to her.

This section will explain how to undertake confidence building as well as how to establish a safe space for her, to improve the chances of success when introducing her to new family members. First, however, is a description on how to litter train a cat; this will be important as a new cat generally needs to stay in the home for around three to four weeks prior to being allowed outside, if she is going to be let out. You should also make sure your cat is neutered and microchipped prior to going outside, to increase her safety and uphold welfare.

Litter training

Cats are often already litter trained, whether they are within a home or currently reside in rescue. However, during introductions to new environments and individuals you may need to re-train the cat. This may be required to actively encourage them to use a particular location, use a new substrate or use a new litter tray, in which case you should follow the guidance in Exercise 1.

Exercise 1: Litter training

- Step 1: Refer to the 'resources' section in Chapter 1 and make sure the environment setup is appropriate.
- Step 2: Encourage her close to and into the tray, using things she finds reinforcing, ideally after mealtimes when she would naturally need to toilet.
- Step 3: Restrict access around the house until litter training is completed. Providing a smaller area with less opportunities to toilet inappropriately will improve success and reduce the chance she practices undesirable behaviour such as inappropriate toileting.
- Step 4: Reward positive interactions with the tray, especially if elimination occurs. Positive reinforcement increases the chances of a behaviour being repeated. In contrast, punishing undesirable behaviour, such as elimination outside of the tray, can break the bond and relationship and can cause a fear of the litter tray, therefore reducing the chance of success.
- Step 5: When elimination in the tray is successful it can be beneficial to leave a small amount of used litter within the tray. This can encourage returning to the area to toilet and is a tool often used for hand-reared kittens. Some cats may not appreciate an unclean tray, however, so individual preference should be considered.
- Step 6: Perseverance and consistency. Continue to work through the steps and reward the desired behaviour and positive interactions, taking note of her preferences as you work through the exercises.

Confidence building

Socialisation is something which should, ideally, be carried out early in a cat's life, as explained earlier, and carried out, where possible, by the initial caregivers such as the breeders or rescue centres. If socialisation has not occurred, then this can cause some cats to be more nervous around novel stimuli. Therefore, exposing cats positively to as many objects, sounds, and social stimuli (cats, dogs and people) as possible, in a controlled manner, is important in improving welfare. Doing this throughout her life can help build confidence, but also increase her resilience and adaptability. This is important, as when bigger changes occur within the household, she will be more likely to adapt to these changes without it affecting her detrimentally or causing any potential undesirable behaviours. Building her confidence can therefore set her up to be more successful to live within a family environment, as well as develop a buffer to change and being around novel stimuli.

Exercise 2 provides guidance on the process of how to build confidence in cats around a variety of stimuli. All exposures, but especially the initial exposures, should be controlled and positive, making sure she remains relaxed during the whole session. It is important, particularly for nervous cats, to present new and potentially scary stimuli at their lowest possible intensity, to ensure that the cat stays under the threshold for stress and does not become scared in their presence. This can be done using a technique called desensitisation, which is where the presentation of the stimuli is reduced by:

1. Increasing the distance between the stimulus and the cat.
2. Lowering the volume of the stimulus, if it has a sound element.
3. Reducing the movement of the stimulus.
4. Presenting the stimulus for a short period of time.

Exercise 2: Building confidence

- Set up the environment to be as stress-free as possible, for instance, having familiar items around her, or being in a safe space with comforting stimuli, but few stressors.

- Add the new stimulus to the environment at a low intensity, so that she is kept under threshold for stress and is not showing any undesirable behaviours such as hiding. Every time the stimulus is presented and throughout the period that the stimulus is present provide a pleasurable high-value food treat such as tuna or cheese. Anytime she shows confident behaviours then you can also encourage this by providing food treats. You can also provide attention that she finds pleasurable such as praise and touch. Make sure you go at her pace and that she controls her distance from the stimulus, and avoid sudden noises or movements that might spook her, particularly during the early exposures.

- Increase the intensity slowly, as long as she continues to remain relaxed in its presence, and only if it is necessary to do so. Continue to pair the stimulus or her relaxed behaviour with the pleasurable stimulus (high value food treat, praise and/or touch).

Top tips

- Some avoidance and stress may be seen, but if she does not eat the food provided and shows continuous avoidance in the presence of the stimuli then you should decrease the intensity of the stimuli in the environment, give her more time to get use to the environment and put more effort into building her confidence in the environment without the additional stimuli/stressors.

- Food is naturally reinforcing, and therefore providing her meal in the presence of the stimuli may also be helpful. If she is startled at any point during this process, then immediately provide her with something pleasant such as increased food treats or attention to encourage her to bounce back to build her resilience. She may not eat the food treats if she is too stressed and hides, but where possible try to end the session on a positive.

Safe spaces

A safe space is a location where the cat feels comfortable and stress free, she can fully relax and access all her desired resources. Whether she is coming into a new house or is currently in a house and having a new member of the family introduced into the household, a safe space should be created for her. Ideally it should be a place of her choice (where possible), where she can be alone and relaxed. This space should be a place that she associates with positive things, and is usually where she is fed or where her bed is located, but it can be any place where she feels fully relaxed and comfortable.

She may choose her own safe space, but you should make sure that this is not a bolthole or somewhere she has typically hidden when scared or showing behaviours indicative of fear. In this scenario she is more likely to remain in a negative state of mind, is less likely to learn new positive associations about her surroundings, and it will therefore be harder to encourage alternative behaviours.

A safe space should be somewhere that she is confident and prefers to relax, and where she can perform typical daily behaviours such as sleeping. It is therefore important for her to have free access to the space. If a space is not selected by her, then you can establish one by encouraging a location where positive things happen; this can be done using respondent and operant conditioning. Exercise 3 provides guidance on the process of how to establish a safe space for a cat. Interactions should be based on how much she wants to interact with you; let her make the choice as to whether to interact or not. Do not force her to interact until she is ready, and just go at her pace, making sure every exposure is positive and enjoyable.

If using food treats, make sure they are motivating and safe for her. If she is completely new to the environment and needs to stay in that space, she may be more nervous, as the whole environment is full of unfamiliar smells and sounds. If she is hiding, then encourage her out of the hiding space with high value rewards while calmly speaking to her gently. If she is too nervous, however, then give her a bit more time alone to explore the environment in her own time. She should always be able to access a place to hide. If she is particularly friendly and confident, and is happy for you to interact, then calmly provide her with attention, food treats and/or you can even engage some gentle play with her, such as chasing a wand toy, as these are all reinforcing and will help her to settle.

Exercise 3: Developing a safe space

- Decide on a location that is out of the way, can be separated from other spaces if necessary, and has reduced stressors. If the cat is already in the environment, then select a space that she chooses to spend time in, if it is somewhere she feels relaxed.

- Place familiar resources into the space which retain the cat's scent. Make sure she has all the required resources such as food, litter tray, water, scratch post, and any additional enrichment. If the environment is completely new for her then make sure you give her some time to explore and build her confidence in the environment in her own time. For a space to be safe it needs to be known and comfortable; a novel space could cause stress in itself. If she is the current cat, and therefore used to the environment, she should be able to come and go from the space, except for the safe space being set up for a new cat, which should be kept separate in these stages. Avoid stressors being able to move into her safe space as well, for example other pets, children or anything that may elevate stress during this time. By engaging in positive behaviours such as facial rubbing, grooming and eating, she will then associate this space as being a positive space to relax.

- Provide lots of high-value food treats in this space while you are present, especially when she shows any investigatory or confident behaviours in the environment or in you. Avoid any sudden noises or movements that may cause her to startle; however, if this does occur provide her with some food treats and give her some time. You are better off sitting comfortably in the space, avoiding hard eye contact, and letting her choose how she wants to engage with you while she builds her confidence. If she actively seeks attention, then you can continue the interaction, but this should be led by her. Withdraw interaction momentarily to observe her behaviour and whether she reinitiates engagement once again. Continue to follow this pattern to allow her time and space to remove herself if she begins to feel uncomfortable or overwhelmed.

- Increase the types of interactions you have with her in the space, such as brushing, playing games with or providing attention to (praise and stroking). Make sure she always perceives the interactions as pleasant and chooses to continue engaging in the activity/interaction.

3: A clowder of cats

This chapter focuses on introducing cats to other cats, whether it is introducing a new cat to one who already lives with you, or introducing a new cat to multiple cats (known as a clowder) – many households have multiple cats living with them. This chapter will cover:

- Assessing the likelihood of whether cats will accept each other
- The best way to prepare the individuals for meeting, to improve the likelihood of successful and harmonious interactions
- How to introduce them
- How to monitor and manage ongoing interactions and troubleshoot potential issues, including how to improve current relationships

Cats can benefit from living with other cats, and often cat lovers choose to have more than one within their homes. Research conducted in catteries has, in fact, demonstrated that sociability can be higher in cats that live with other cats. Other research has found that stress levels do not differ in single- and multi-cat households; however, this is likely to be influenced by the environmental setup, as well as how the cats have been introduced.

There are many factors, however, that can influence a cat's sociability, such as whether they have lived with other adult cats since being a kitten and whether they are provided with relevant resources, as detailed in Chapter 1. The individuals, their experiences, their personality and behavioural traits need to be considered prior to introducing cats. As they are 'selectively social', it is not guaranteed they will get on with all the cats they are introduced to. However, if processes are followed, it can increase the success of future interactions. Figure 3.1 demonstrates

Cats can benefit from living in multi-cat households.

Stage	Exercise	Measure of success	Record of progress
Upon success at each stage you can progress to the next stage. However, if there are any difficulties, look at the troubleshooting guide and/or move back a stage.			*Example: the current cat shows some frustration at not being able to get access to the new cat's safe space.*
Stage one: Create safe spaces	3 (and 2)	Both cats are relaxed and carrying out a range of natural behaviours in their spaces, such as grooming, playing, resting.	
Stage two: Scent swapping	4	As above	
Stage three: Feeding in view of each other	5	The cats are eating without a barrier, while only glancing at each other occasionally	
Stage four: Introduction	6	The cats are mostly relaxed and perform natural behaviours in each others' presence. There is no conflict between them.	

Figure 3.1. The process to follow when introducing two or more cats.

the process to follow when introducing cats to each other. You can use this as a record of your progress, and where you struggle to progress at any stage you should seek guidance from the troubleshooting figures (3.3, 3.4 and 3.5) found in this chapter. This chapter will provide details on how to progress through the stages of introducing cats in the most successful manner. First, however, the cats being introduced should be assessed.

3.1 Feline friends

If you know which cats will be introduced to each other then you should have completed Feline Assessment 1 on both cats, as described from Chapter 2. Remember that if either cat is a true feral under two months old, or a non-feral under four months old, they should be instantly scored as green. If either is a feral older than two months old or a non-feral over four months old, your assessment results (red, amber, or green) will indicate which approach to take regarding introductions as well as what preparations should be undertaken beforehand, as shown in Figure 3.2. These scores make predictions on the likelihood of success for the individuals involved, and what adjustments might help improve the chances of success. You should, however, be mindful of what caused her to score how she did, such as whether she has shown fear responses or does not adapt well to new situations. When setting up the environments and introducing the individuals, act with caution to reduce the likelihood of her becoming stressed, for instance doing more confidence building (Exercise 2). If the cat is not currently neutered, this should be considered prior to the introduction (unless she is too young), and both cats should be sufficiently vaccinated and prophylactically treated for parasites.

If you have not yet selected your new cat, it's best to seek advice from the place you are getting your cat from, for example the rescue centre or breeder, who would have assessed the likely sociability of cats in their care. You may also wish to share the exercise with them to help support the scoring. If you are introducing multiple cats, you should complete the assessment for all individuals being introduced, and follow the guidance for the cats that have the worst scores.

Proceed: Where both cats result in green scores, it is okay to proceed with the introduction process as described within the chapter. It is still important to consider that some cats just may not live together well, and having two green scoring cats does not guarantee smooth and successful interactions consistently.

Score for current cat \ Score for new cat	Green	Amber	Red
Green	Proceed	Proceed with caution	Stop and think
Amber	Proceed with caution	Proceed with caution	Stop and think
Red	Stop and think	Stop and think	Do not proceed

Figure 3.2. Using the FSP scores for both the current cat and the new cat you can see which approach you should take prior to introducing the cats to each other.

Proceed with caution: Where one or both cats result in an amber score, you should proceed with caution. This would mean that you should be prepared to:

- Provide both cats with more time to develop their safe spaces and relax in the environment, particularly the new cat, as well as more time to prepare for the introductions and when progressing through the next stages of the process.
- Consider using pheromonal diffusers to assist.

The time provision considered will vary depending on whether any of the cats scored amber, as well as their individual personalities. It is important that you monitor behaviours and responses sufficiently and only move to the next stage once you are comfortable the cats are ready.

Stop and think: Where one of the cats has been given a red score then you should stop and think, considering if this cat is going to settle. This is particularly important if the red scorer is the cat already in the household; if they are not confident or resilient in their current environment, additional stressors may impact their welfare. Your cat should feel safe and secure within their home as this provides them with the foundation to be receptive to change and adapt accordingly. You should therefore consider whether these are the right individuals to introduce to one another, or whether another cat is the right choice at this time. If the introduction is unavoidable, extra care needs to be taken when setting up a safe space and carrying out the introductions. It is important to improve the chances of success where possible by taking things slowly, and you should expect that it may take a lot longer to succeed. You should also be prepared that she may never fully accept the integration and therefore her welfare will need to be continuously monitored. Where possible:

- Provide both cats with more time to develop their safe spaces and relax in the environment, particularly the new

cat, as well as more time to prepare for the introductions and when progressing through the next stages of the process.
- Carry out Exercise 2 to build the confidence of the red-scoring cat prior to moving to the next stages.
- Use pheromonal diffusers to assist.

Do not proceed: Where both cats score red, then the advice would be not to proceed with the introduction, as they are unlikely to be suitable to live together and it may be detrimental to their overall welfare. It could be more successful to introduce the red-scoring cat to one that scores as green or amber. Instead, you could spend more time trying to building the cat's confidence using Exercise 2 before attempting an introduction.

3.2 Environment

The first part of preparation is to make sure the environment is set up for success. This includes providing enough resources to prevent cats fighting over beds, latrine areas, food and toys, as well as providing enough space so that they can take themselves away from the other cats in the house. If the environment has plenty of resources available for each cat that lives there, most cats will happily live alongside each other, or they will at least tolerate each other. First exposures to new resources, new spaces/environments, and new individuals should always be very calm and positive with very little interactions during this period unless initiated by either cat. You should also make sure there are very few stressors in the environment.

A pheromone diffuser could be used within the environment before and during the early exposures to new environments or resources to provide a calming influence on the cat. There are also specific pheromone diffusers that can be used prior to and during introductions of cats. Plug-ins can be used in 'high traffic' areas and sprays used on resting and scratching areas around the home. These artificial pheromones mimic those within the facial glands of the cat, as discussed in Chapter 1, and are a tool used to reduce stress and anxiety. It should be noted, however, that these should not be used as a 'quick fix' for behavioural concerns or introductions. They should be used in a complementary manner alongside the exercises and additional management techniques. The use of pheromonal diffusers may be particularly important if an amber or red scoring cat is involved in the introductions.

Resources

Whether you are getting a new cat or already have multiple cats within your home, you need to make sure you have enough resources for every individual, as described in Chapter 2. There are certain essential requirements required for each cat, such as having scratch posts, feeding and water stations, sleeping areas/beds and litter trays, but the more options they have the better, particularly for indoor cats. The ideal for litter trays would be to have one per individual cat plus an extra one, so if you have three cats you should have four litter trays. The resources for the new cat should be provided in their safe space when this is being set up and should mostly include resources with their own scent on. Resident cats should have free access to their own resources which ideally should not have been moved around, to make sure the disruption to their environment is as minimal as possible.

Space

Space is a key area of consideration when looking at welfare, and it is therefore an important aspect to review when introducing cats. Looking at how space can be managed and utilised appropriately by both cats will provide a positive starting point for introductions, and can prevent setting them up for failure. It can be difficult to manage and increase the amount of space available within an existing environment, however there are options, as discussed in Chapter 1. Cats will usually find their own preferred locations however, particularly during introductions, space needs to be managed and orchestrated carefully to maximise success. A lack of safe space and resources are key causes of frustration; which will often lead to conflict and other undesirable behaviours.

When first introducing a new cat to an environment it should be done in as positive and stress-free a manner as possible. It is important for each cat to be able to access space away from the other cat when they need it. A separate safe space should be created for each cat prior to the introductions, particularly for new cats to allow them to settle within their new environment. These should be established using Exercise 3 in Chapter 2.

Resident cats should have access to the house as they normally do, except for the space that is being created for the new cat. You do not need to change too much of their setup or routine, and you should disrupt their space as little as possible, ideally choosing the new cat's space to be one that the current cat does not use as much or is not their preference. Where this is not possible, make sure you

Resident cats should be able to engage in their normal activities and routines to disrupt them as little as possible.

When cats scent mark by rubbing the side of their cheek on items within the environment, it is a sign that they are becoming more settled.

create an alternate safe space for them as well, with access to outdoor space, if they already have that, to reduce the impact on them.

For the new cat it is important that you keep the current cat out of this space, and ideally avoid them seeing each other for the first few days, at least. This will allow the new cat to build positive associations within this space and establish it as a safe place, as well as allow them to settle in their new environment away from additional stressors. Once a cat has begun to investigate her surroundings and has started rubbing her cheek on items within the environment, this can be a sign that she is becoming more settled. Once she is feeling more relaxed, she will likely engage in behaviours including play. If space is an issue within the home environment, and additional resources and safe spaces cannot be included, it may be worth considering whether adding another cat into the household is the most suitable action at this time. If they do not settle in the space, consider using a pheromonal diffuser for longer and/or give more time for them to settle, increasing pleasant interactions and increasing the high value rewards.

When a cat is relaxed and feels comfortable in her environment she is more likely to play.

3.3 Learning

Once both cats have settled into their safe spaces, the next stage will be to begin the introduction of the cats. This should first start with scent swapping, and then you can gradually build up to the cats being visible to each other until finally they can be sharing the same spaces. Throughout this process you should always be thinking about how you build the cat's confidence, particularly when around the other cat, and continue to encourage relaxed behaviours.

Scent swapping

A familiar scent to a cat is important in reducing stress, so swapping scents between the cats is an important stage in the process of introducing the individuals to each other. Exercise 4 identifies different options as to how you can swap scents between the two cats and their safe spaces.

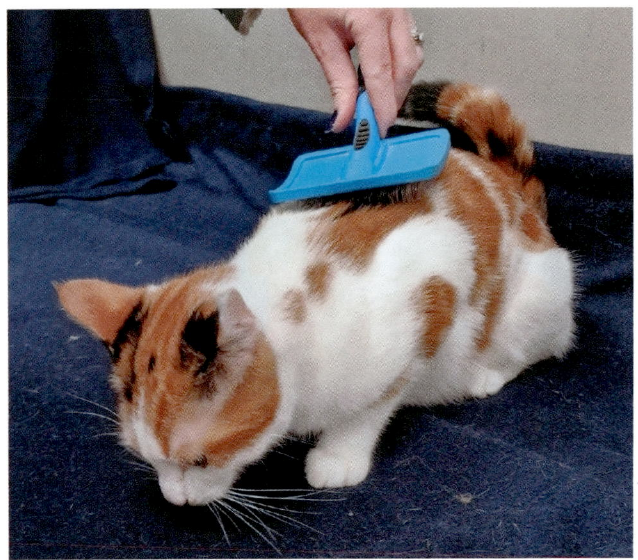

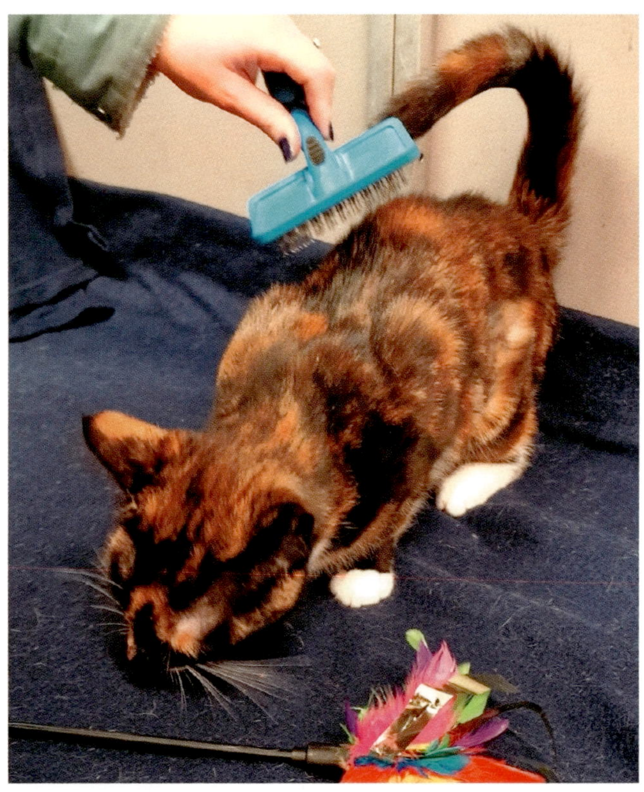

Brush both cats with the same brush, one after the other, to swap their scents. Only do this if they enjoy being brushed.

Feed the cats on opposite sides of a door (or a temporary barrier, as here) in the new cat's safe space.

Exercise 4: Scent swapping

- If the cat likes to be brushed, you should start by brushing each of the cats with the same brush to create a communal scent between them, or move between each cat, stroking them one after the other. If either cat does not enjoy being brushed or stroked, focus on swapping toys or other resources.
- Feed the cats on the opposite sides of a closed door so that they can smell each other while they are feeding, this may need to be done at a bit of a distance from the door dependent on the individuals involved. The new cat should be in their safe space while the current cat can be on the other side of the door.
- Start swapping resources that the cats have interacted with, such as toys. Make sure you just swap one item at a time into each other's safe space so that it is not too overwhelming, and interact with the items in a positive manner, such as playing or by pairing the items presence with some food treats. This is so that they associate the item and its scent with something pleasant.
- Continue to swap the scents between the cats for a few days while the cats are separate. Once they are quite relaxed during this process you can also begin to let the new cat access the rest of the house for short periods of time to explore the different scents and wider environment, although don't let the cats meet at this stage. Make sure you allow the new cat to explore in their own time, but you can provide lots of reinforcement. This is often best done if your current cat/s are outside (if they are already outdoor cats) and are unlikely to bump into each other. If they are both indoor cats, this may be more difficult unless you can let the new cat explore while the other cat rests in a different part of the house. During this time, you can let the new cat enter the rest of the house for exploration. During this process make sure your new cat does not become too overwhelmed, and continue to provide some positive reinforcement.

Top tips

- You should continue to brush all cats with the same brush throughout the next few stages of the introduction process.

Feeding in view

Although this can be classed as an interaction, the purpose is to begin to teach the cats that there is enough food and space available, and that they can eat in safety around each other. After the new cat is settled in the environment and a period of scent swapping, you should start feeding them in each other's presence to encourage calm behaviours while they can see each other.

In Exercise 5 you will be pairing the sight of the other cat with something pleasant, which should inadvertently build their confidence when in the other cat's presence. You can use their actual dinner but it is more beneficial to use a variety of high value food treats instead. If there are more than two cats being introduced to each other make sure you have multiple people to help provide food treats and attention to all the cats, and just take it more slowly and take more care.

Both cats should be kept under the threshold for stress, and although they may initially show some discomfort this should be kept to a minimum. Some signs of discomfort around feeding include flattened ears which are sideways on the head, vigilant behaviour around food and reluctance to consume food. If there are any issues with the implementation of this exercise, see Figure 3.3 for troubleshooting.

Exercise 5: Feeding in view

- Start at a distance far enough away so that they do not become highly aroused or stressed. This distance will be dependent on each cat and situation, and you can use a transparent barrier or ideally have an individual with each cat to provide high value food treats and attention. Both cats should ideally be in or near their safe spaces and at a comfortable distance where they will both eat. You may need to provide high value food treats. They should be allowed to move away if they choose, but if they do you may need to go back a stage or give them more time to build up their confidence.

- The cats should be positively reinforced with extra food treats and attention (stroking, praise) to encourage both cats to stay calm and relaxed. Encourage positive emotional states and promote confident responses and purring. When they see each other relaxed in their presence, they are likely to not see each other as a threat. If either begins to look tense or fixate too much on the other cat, redirect their attention onto something else and increase the distance between them where necessary, but make sure it remains positive. Increasing the value of the reinforcer (food treat) may also be useful to reduce increasing arousal.

- Make sure you keep these sessions short and end on a positive before separating them again.

- This should be done a few times, and the more times you do it the more she will feel comfortable in the other cat's presence. You can then build up to where they can see each other during mealtimes as well, but not until they are relaxed in each other's presence while eating high value food treats at a distance. You can also slowly decrease the distance between the cats, if necessary, but you should continuously observe both cats' behaviours throughout, and only progress if both cats are mostly relaxed.

- The cats may just tolerate each other, and they may prefer to keep their distance. There may be a bit of hissing if one cat gets too close, but so long as nothing escalates just make sure that you keep it all positive and keep providing reinforcement. Let the cats listen to each other, respond appropriately, and learn each other's boundaries; it will take some time, but just intervene and refocus where necessary.

Top tips

- The cats should always have the space to be able to increase the distance between themselves, so that they can move away from each other and into their safe spaces.

- Do not begin this when they are particularly hungry as they may become more easily frustrated in each other's presence.

- Providing the high value food treats only on these occasions may help them make the association quicker between the sight of the other cat and the treats, and therefore learn more quickly that the other cat is not a threat.

- Never allow the cats to steal each other's food as this will create conflict: they need to know that there are enough resources to share.

Issues	Action
If a cat will not eat in the presence of the other cat.	Go back a stage and continue scent swapping, making them feel comfortable and confident in their own spaces, as well as trying to let them investigate each other's spaces without meeting. When you do come to let them see each other at a distance again make sure the distance has been increased, where possible, or use a higher value reinforcer. For the cat that is not eating, place the food treats higher up off the floor and consider using a pheromonal diffuser to make her more relaxed. Use alternative reinforcers, such as giving her attention by stroking or brushing, or doing alternative activities such as playing her favourite game. If you use games, then focus on only using low arousal games where the cat is not darting about too quickly and over too much distance. Try to avoid using games in the first few interactions if possible.
If one of the cats is particularly nervous and actively avoids the other.	You can place the nervous cat's food treats higher up so that she feels safer being off the floor, particularly when there are multiple cats, dogs and/or children around. Take more time to build the cat's confidence while the other cat is out of sight, and then build it up while keeping the other cat at a distance.

Figure 3.3. Troubleshooting for Exercise 5, identifying some of the issues and how to action them. If any don't work then go back a stage and focus on doing more confidence building.

- Whenever they are in each other's presence, make sure the environment stays calm and that you provide plenty of reinforcement in the form of nice food treats or attention such as stroking, as long as this is something they enjoy.
- They are likely to keep a distance, but if one approaches the other keep an eye on their responses. Avoid negative interactions and actively try to distract the more confident cat, especially if you feel the other cat is struggling and showing signs of nervousness. Avoid it getting to the point where either cat

Feed the cats a little way apart, but still in each other's sight. This should start at a comfortable distance where both cats will eat.

needs to hiss if possible, but if either do just distract them, increase the distance between them and reinforce them.

- Separate feeding spaces and resources should always be available, even if interactions have been positive.

The cats are relaxed in each other's presence while investigating and playing with a toy.

Relaxed cats sharing the same space.

3.4 Interactions

There should be a natural progression from the cats having built their confidence, being fed in view of each other, to further interactions (from Exercises 5 and 6). After completing Exercise 5 until they are comfortable being and eating in each other's presence, so you can begin to let them enter each other's spaces to investigate. It is important during this stage to monitor their behaviours carefully and manage the environment so that the cats can be in control of their distance, but for both to feel as comfortable as possible. During these exposures you should provide both cats with appropriate guidance to encourage calm investigation and avoid all undesirable behaviours.

If there are more than two cats being introduced to each other, make sure you have multiple people to help provide food treats and attention to all the cats, or introduce two individuals at a time. Make sure you take introductions a lot slower, making sure you put in the groundwork first and observe all the cats' behaviours carefully. Cats may demonstrate some undesired behaviours towards each other, such as hissing; the aim should be to avoid these behaviours wherever possible, and instead progress slowly, always maintaining positive emotional states and interactions to avoid undesirable associations occurring. For this stage you should use Exercise 6, and if there are any issues, see Figure 3.4 for troubleshooting.

Issues	Action
If either cat hisses, spits or swipes at the other cat.	Distract them both with lots of nice things to de-arouse both cats and increase the distance between them. Remove one cat immediately if you are particularly worried about an escalation. Go back a stage if necessary to scent swapping, but if you are able to distract them both then that is a positive and maybe continue with seeing each other at a further distance being fed their normal meals and high value treats where necessary to build their confidence around each other.
If the cats start fighting and/or chasing each other.	Make sure the chase behaviour is not play. If it is but it is inappropriate then you should focus on playing with the individual in a different manner and provide them with lots of enrichment and some training to reduce their focus on the other cat. Distract (using a loud sound to startle if necessary) and separate the cats and then go back to the first stage doing more confidence building, more scent sharing, reducing arousal and conditioning (providing lots of pleasant food treats or attention). You should progress very slowly and focus initially on the cats being in each others presence or around each others scent before progressing to avoid any further agonistic situations as these will make it harder to progress.
If either cat becomes negatively emotionally aroused or become stressed.	Focus on distracting the cats, redirecting their arousal onto toys and/or reducing arousal. You may need to increase the distance between them or separate them for a short while to de-arouse them.
If either cat is showing any signs of pseudo spraying (as though they are about to urine mark).	Provide more scratching locations and encourage alternative scent depositing behaviours such as running their cheeks on furniture, items and your hands. This will de-arouse them and help them to feel more confident within the environment.

Figure 3.4. Troubleshooting for Exercise 6, identifying some of the issues that may occur, and how to action them. If any don't work then go back a stage and focus on doing more confidence building.

Exercise 6: Enhanced introductions

- Open all the doors, including to the safe spaces to allow free access for both cats to roam freely. Try and do this when the current cat is already relaxing. The cats do not need to be encouraged into specific locations and should instead be left to move around freely. You should not intervene except for providing food treats and positive attention to both cats separately.

- You should focus on actively providing them both with high value treats, brushing them, providing them with attention such as stroking and playing games together. Let them approach, sniff and interact with each other in their own time but when they do meet keep arousal levels low with some gentle strokes and high value food treats which can be dropped on the floor. Talk to the cats as well in a calm manner. If they approach each other and sniff, make sure you continue to keep them calm and reinforce their behaviour. Sometimes if cats sniff each other for too long it can lead to anxiety therefore provide them with high value food rewards to avoid this. To avoid interactions becoming negative you can also distract the more confident cat and redirect their attention elsewhere.

- Once they are mostly settled in each other's presence and their behaviours around each other are more predictable, even if they still show some avoidance of each other or hissing, you can begin to move some of their resources (scratch posts, litter trays) to more desired places. You should however be careful not to do this too soon and try and do this gradually, where possible.

- Only leave them alone together when you can trust there will not be conflict between them, and they are relaxed in each other's presence.

Top tips

- Avoid quick or sudden movements in these early stages as the cats are likely to be cautious anyway. However, over time, the more relaxed they become in each other's presence, you can begin play with them, starting with some low arousal chasing of toys.

- You may want to use the highest value food treats for close interactions.

- Do not allow the cats to chase each other.

- Avoid allowing chasing of each other unless it is obvious play behaviour; however, true play is unlikely to happen between two unfamiliar adult cats straight away.

- You cannot use enough high value treats during an interaction or meeting. Giving them their meals when they can see each other at a distance is great at building their confidence in each other's presence.

- If either cat gets aroused, make sure it is not driven by a negative emotional state, as described in Chapter 2, and is not making the other cat uncomfortable. If it is, you may need to manage arousal levels to avoid this.

3.5 Dynamics

It is important to continuously monitor the ongoing interactions and welfare of both cats, using the information provided in Chapter 2 on how to interpret their behaviour. It may be normal for the occasional hiss or chase, but where you feel that the behaviour of one of the cats is indicative of stress, and she is hiding a lot more or suppressing her natural behaviours, you may need to move back a stage in the process and refer to the troubleshooting guide (Figure 3.5). It is beneficial to avoid frustrations where possible, and continue to use positive reinforcement for desirable behaviours and to promote harmonious interactions.

If it is difficult to manage interactions due to inappropriate play or agonistic behaviour, you should consider the welfare of both cats in this scenario, especially if you have tried troubleshooting, taken your time throughout the process, and the environment cannot be adjusted significantly to allow for better progression. If during any of this process, you are concerned for welfare or behaviour of one of the cats, or you see very little progression in being able to integrate them safely, check their health before continuing, in case there is an underlying cause. You could contact the place where you got the cat for advice, or contact an accredited feline behaviourist for further specialist support.

Issues	Action
One cat is too playful or inappropriate during play.	Redirect their play onto toys and provide them with a range of alternative enrichment to keep them occupied and reduce their energy. While playing with the cat keep them separate from the other cat while they expel their energy. Encourage calm behaviours around the other cat, for instance by doing some training with the playful cat. Provide reinforcement to the cat for making right choices.
One of the cat starts urine spraying.	Figure out what the trigger is, whether it is true urination or marking behaviour. If you are not sure then try a range of the actions below. If it is marking behaviour then avoid the trigger and provide alternative scent marking opportunities such as facial rubbing and scratch posts. If true urination, re-house-train the cat and change the litter tray options, for instance using different types of litter trays, substrates or locations.
If the current cat tries to gain access to the new cat's safe space.	Provide with alternative space, where possible, make other spaces more interesting for the cat and provide additional enrichment and mental stimulation.
One of the cats is very nervous and actively avoids and hides constantly.	Go back to scent swapping and do more confidence building in the nervous cat before starting to feed the cats in view. If the nervous cat gets approached by the other cat, the other one should be redirected and provided with attention away from the nervous cat.
If one cat becomes fixated on the other cat.	Go back a stage, increase the distance between them, give them more time, and try and find alternative reinforcers that may be higher value.

Figure 3.5. General troubleshooting, identifying some of the other issues that may occur during the process and how to action them. If any don't work then go back a stage and focus on doing more confidence building.

4: Cats and canines

This chapter focuses on introducing cats to dogs. For ease of reading the dog will be referred to as he/him throughout. Cats and dogs can usually live together successfully, and here we will cover:

- Assessing the likelihood of whether the cat and dog are likely to accept each other
- The best way to prepare the individuals for meeting to improve the likelihood of successful and harmonious interactions
- How to introduce them for the best success
- How to monitor and manage ongoing interactions and troubleshoot potential issues, including how to improve existing relationships

Cats and dogs can benefit from living together.

Cats and dogs can have close relationships that may benefit both individuals. Cats that have successfully lived with dogs before are more likely to accept living with dogs, and the same vice versa, however this doesn't mean that inexperienced individuals can't accept living together. The individuals, their experiences, their personality and behavioural traits need to be considered prior to introductions, because if cats are flighty and/or if dogs are likely to chase cats, then this is more likely to affect the success of the introduction.

Figure 4.1 demonstrates the process to follow when introducing a cat to a dog. You can use this as a record of your progress, and where you struggle to progress at any stage you should seek guidance from troubleshooting Figure 4.6. This chapter will provide details on how to progress through the stages of introducing a cat and dog in the most successful manner. However, first the individuals should both be assessed.

Stage	Exercise	Measure of success	Record of progress
Upon success at each stage you can progress to the next stage. However, if there are any difficulties, look at troubleshooting and/or move back a stage.			*Example: the dog consistently barks in the cat's presence.*
Stage one: Create safe spaces	3 (and 2)	The cat and dog are both relaxed and will carry out a range of natural behaviours in their environment, such as playing, resting and eating.	
Stage two: Dog training	7	The dog will lie down on a bed and will remain settled and calm while intermittently being fed.	
	8	The dog will focus on you when requested to do so.	
	9	The dog will come back to you immediately upon request.	
	10	The dog will release a toy or chew upon request.	
Stage three: Introduction	11	The dog and cat are calm and relaxed in each others' presence. They will both eat food and, over time, will increase the amount of natural behaviours they perform, eg investigation, resting. There is no conflict between them.	
Stage four: Introduction	6	The cats are mostly relaxed and perform natural behaviours in each others' presence. There is no conflict between them.	

Figure 4.1. The process to follow when introducing a cat to a dog.

4.1 Feline friends

Cats can be very territorial, and the physical environment is important to a cat with even small changes sometimes affecting her behaviour, such as when new furniture is placed in the environment or when furniture has been moved around a room, which may trigger scent marking and investigation. There are considerations to take when bringing a cat into a dog's environment, or when bringing a dog into a cat's environment.

When a dog is being introduced to a cat's environment it is not only a big change for the cat, but it can also be quite scary and stressful, particularly if she has not had positive experiences around dogs before or if she has not lived in a multi-pet household before. There will suddenly be areas of her territory that she may now be cautious about exploring, and her access may need to be managed for a period.

If the cat is the pet being brought into a household that already has a dog, then everything will be new to her, so her exposures to the environment should be gradual. In this scenario you need to ensure that the existing dog is already used to having areas within the home restricted, so that a safe space can be established for the cat.

Ideally, cats should be confident and relaxed and dogs should be calm for successful introductions. It is generally easier when a dog is more nervous of the cat than a cat is of the dog, but it is important that both are stress-free and therefore the right preparations need to be carried out first. By completing assessments on both individuals, we can make predictions on the likelihood of success for all involved. If you have not yet selected the new individual to the household, then seek advice from the place where you are getting them, regarding the likely sociability and suitability of the individuals within their care. If you are introducing multiple cats or multiple dogs, then you should complete the assessments for all individuals being introduced, and follow the guidance for the cats and dogs that have the worst scores.

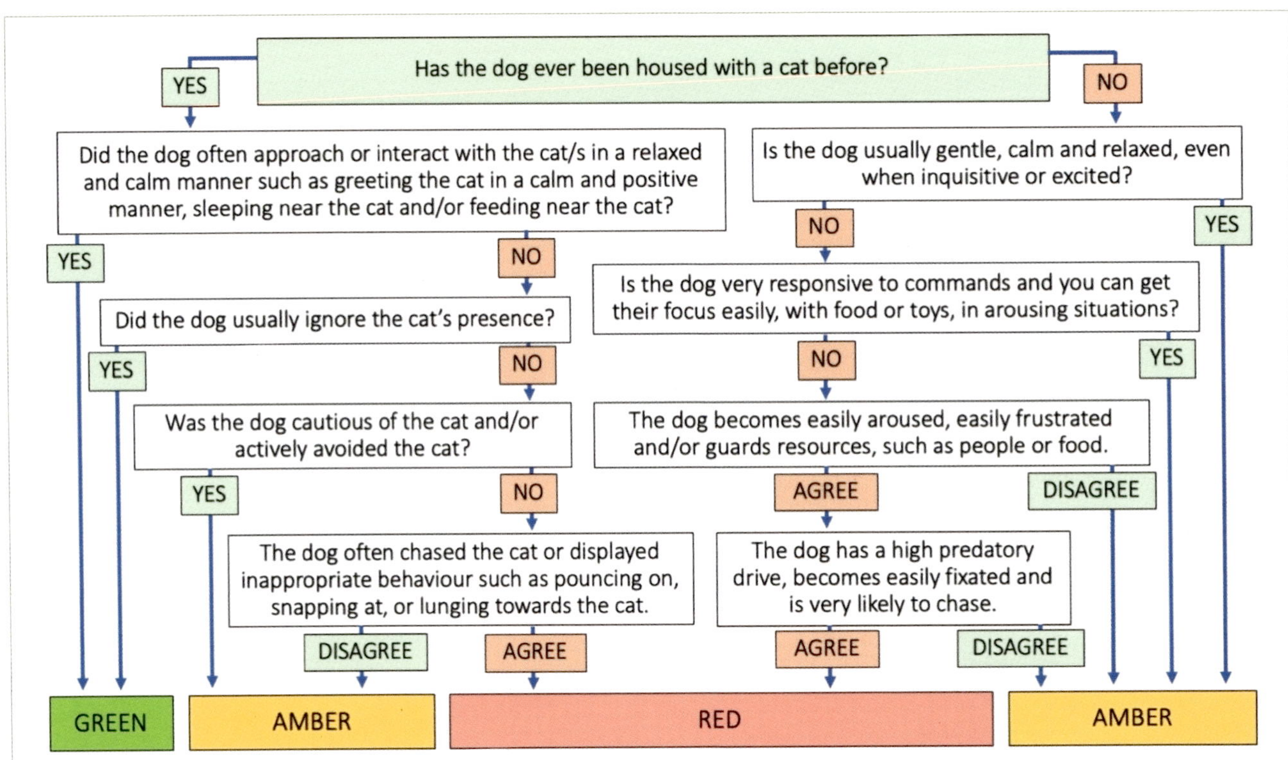

Figure 4.2. The canine assessment, which assesses the dog's potential suitability to live with cats. If you are unsure on any of the answers, choose 'No' or 'Agree'.

A cat and dog interacting in a relaxed and appropriate manner.

Canine assessment

As with cats, there are a range of factors that influence how a dog will respond in a situation. A dog that has previous experience living with cats is more likely to be successful when introduced to a new cat; however, the dog's behaviour will indicate the type of experience he has had around cats and whether they have been positive or negative for him. A puppy under four months old should be considered as green.

Prior to introductions, the canine assessment (Figure 4.2) should be completed by the person who spends most time with the dog or knows the dog best. The assessment consists of questions and statements about the dog's previous social experiences with other cats, as well as behavioural tendencies and personality traits, based on his overall responses in everyday situations and to changes in the environment. If the question or statement applies to the

Below: A cat and dog relaxed and calm in each other's presence.

dog in some situations but not others, you'll need to make a judgement as to how much you agree or disagree in the provision of your answer. Complete them all as best as you can but if you are unsure about any of the answers or if his prior experiences are unknown then just answer either *'No'* or *'Agree'*.

This assessment is much more about the individual dog than the breed; however, it is also important to take his size into consideration. Larger dogs *may* appear more threatening to a cat than smaller breeds, and this should not be overlooked. Consider how a bouncy and energetic large dogs come across, against a toy breed for example.

Dogs that are relaxed will be floppy and loose in their movements and expressions. A dog that becomes tense maybe cautious or may have increased arousal due to positive or negative affect. When a dog shows tolerance towards a cat, he mostly ignores the cat's presence and is not particularly interested in interacting with the cat. He may also prefer to maintain a certain distance between himself and the cat, particularly if he is of a somewhat cautious character. If overly excited he could be keen to investigate and interact with the cat and may be rather bouncy. If he becomes frustrated, he is likely to show a range of behaviours including barking and lunging, whereas if he shows a predatory response, he is likely to fixate on the cat by staring intensely at her, his body posture going tense and leaning forwards before launching into a chase. In both cases it is difficult to distract his attention away from the cat and he is highly likely to chase the cat.

High arousal is a state of heightened physical and emotional energy, and is very context specific. Arousal can be triggered when a dog is in a negative emotional state, such as when he becomes frustrated about not achieving a desired outcome, or when he is in a positive emotional state, such as during play or when he is excited. Arousal is also more likely when he is around new people, animals or in new environments, when he has had a lack of exercise and during social interactions. When a dog is highly aroused, he is

	A dog that becomes fearful or frustrated around the cat or during interactions.	**A dog that gets over excited when around the cat or during an interaction.**
Prevention	Take your dog for a walk or play with your dog to reduce energy levels prior to training, social introductions and/or situations that may trigger arousal.	
	Avoid situations that your dog is scared of, or manage access to resources to avoid triggering frustration. Do training to build the dog's confidence and/or to build the dog's frustration tolerance.	Provide a range of enrichment and resources, in the form of food treats, chews and/or toys. Do training to re-focus the dog's attention onto you and encourage an alternative calm behaviour.
Management	Change the interaction or provide an alternative choice of activity, such as letting the dog go outside, taking the dog for a walk, or doing some calm training such as encouraging a settle. It may also be worthwhile increasing the distance to the cat (particularly if the cat is the trigger for the arousal).	
	Provide a range of pleasant resources, such as a high-value food treat, chew or toy, to distract the dog's attention (particularly if frustration driven). Encourage your dog into their safe space (particularly if fear driven).	Redirect the dog's excitement onto something more appropriate, such as a toy (this may need to be quite high-value). Encourage the dog to be excited and/or play in another space that is away from the cat.

Figure 4.3. Some tips on how to prevent high arousal occurring in dogs and how to manage high arousal that may become problematic during interactions.

more likely to demonstrate behaviours that are inappropriate around cats. Arousal can grow quite quickly, and some initial signs may include increased staring, increased panting and an increase in vocalisations such as whimpering or whining. This may then lead to increased movements such as pawing, pouncing, pacing, chasing, snapping the air, and an increased range of vocalisations including barking. Some of these behaviours may be part of an aggressive response due to his emotional state. Even if these behaviours are not directly aimed towards the cat, they can still cause fear and therefore want to be avoided during the introductions.

Increased arousal may be inevitable in some situations, such as during play, but if a dog is likely to become very easily aroused in general, this is likely to have an impact on the cat's welfare. Therefore, it is important to do additional training with the dog prior to an introduction to prevent frequent high arousal, and it is also important to be able to manage his arousal when it does increase (Figure 4.3).

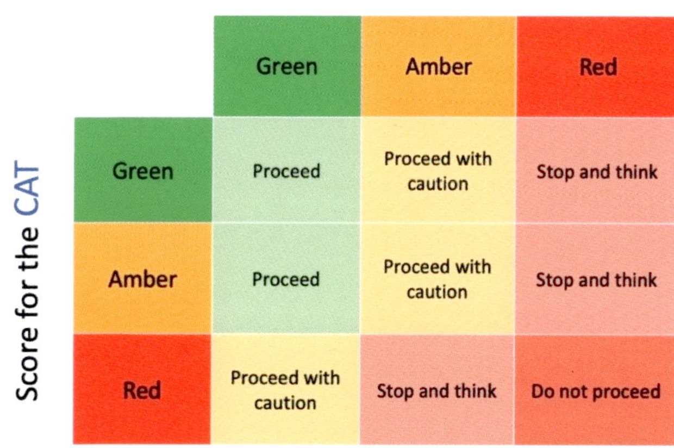

Score for the DOG / Score for the CAT

Score for the CAT \ Score for the DOG	Green	Amber	Red
Green	Proceed	Proceed with caution	Stop and think
Amber	Proceed	Proceed with caution	Stop and think
Red	Proceed with caution	Stop and think	Do not proceed

Figure 4.4. Using the scores for both the cat and the dog you can see which approach you should take prior to introducing them together.

Feline and canine compatibility

A cat that has had previous experience of living with other dogs or has had positive experiences living in multi-pet environments is more likely to be accepting of a dog within the household.

The cat should be assessed and given a feline sociability predictor (FSP) score, using Feline Assessment 2 from Chapter 2. Remember if the cat is a true feral under two months old or a non-feral under four months old, then she is instantly scored as green. If she is a feral older than two months old or a non-feral over four months old, then you should complete the assessment. It is important to be mindful, however, that the instant green assumes there have been no negative experiences. If you are aware of situations which may have been negative for your kitten, then work through the assessment as if she is older, providing you with a greater level of accuracy with regards to her traffic light colour.

Guidance on how to progress, based on both the cat's and dog's scores, is provided in Figure 4.4. This guidance includes how to prepare the individuals to help improve the chances of success. You should, however, be mindful of what caused the individuals to score how they did (red, amber or green) so that when setting up the environment and introducing the individuals, you act with caution to reduce the likelihood of either becoming stressed or demonstrating behaviours that may impact on the success of the introduction.

Proceed: Where the dog gets a green score while the cat scores green or amber, it is okay to proceed with the introduction process as described within this chapter. It is important to still consider that additional training may benefit both individuals to increase the likelihood of a smooth and successful introduction.

Proceed with caution: Where the dog scores green while the cat scores red, both score amber, or the dog scores amber while the cat scores green, you should proceed with caution. Throughout the process, you should also do the following:

- Give the cat more time to develop her confidence within her safe space and/or during scent swapping

- Spend extra time doing the required training with the dog to encourage calm responses, so that you are better able to manage his arousal during the introduction
- Provide more time to prepare for the introductions and when progressing through the next stages of the process
- Consider using pheromonal diffusers to assist in modifying the cat's perception and encourage calm behaviours

The time provision will vary depending on the individuals' personalities. It is important to monitor behaviours and responses sufficiently and only move to the next stage once you are comfortable that both are ready.

Stop and think: Where the cat has scored red while the dog has scored amber, or the dog has scored red while the cat has scored green or amber, you should stop and think. This is particularly important if the red-scoring cat is the existing member of the household; if she is not confident or resilient in her present environment additional stressors may impact her welfare. Your cat should feel safe and secure within her home, as this provides her with the foundation to be receptive to change and adapt accordingly. You should consider whether these are the right individuals to introduce to one another or whether another individual would be the right choice at this time. If the introduction is unavoidable, then extra care needs to be taken while carrying out the following step:

- Give the cat more time to develop her confidence within her safe space and/or during scent swapping
- Spend extra time doing the required training with the dog to encourage calm responses, so that you are better able to manage the dog's arousal during the introduction
- Provide more time to prepare for the introductions and take things slowly when progressing through the stages
- Use pheromonal diffusers to assist.

Although these steps are the same as given under 'Proceed with caution' extra time will probably be necessary in these cases, and will vary depending on the individuals' personalities. Monitor behaviours and responses sufficiently and only move to the next stage once you are comfortable that both are ready.

It may take longer to see success and you should be prepared that the individuals may never fully accept the integration and therefore the welfare of both individuals should be continuously monitored.

Do not proceed: Where both the cat and dog get red scores, the advice would be not to proceed with the introduction. They are unlikely to be suitable to live together and therefore introducing them may be detrimental to their overall welfare. This is especially the case if the dog has been housed with cats before and has shown inappropriate behaviour towards the cat such as fixating intensely on the cat, snapping at or chasing the cat. It would be more likely to be successful if an existing red-scoring individual was introduced to a green-scoring individual. However, if the existing red-scoring animal is a dog, a lot of training will need to be done with him beforehand, to make the introduction safe.

Important consideration for dogs that score red

High arousal is more dangerous if it is predatory or caused by frustration. If a dog is excited and playfully aroused, this can be more successfully managed going forward. If the dog has shown relentless and extreme persistence in his desire to chase the cats that he has previously been housed with, and/or has consistently demonstrated inappropriate behaviours, such as snapping at the cat, then you should not introduce him to a cat. If a dog's predatory drive is strong it is also important not to leave the dog with a cat until you are confident that they will both settle and that his behaviour around the cat is predictable.

Some dogs live peacefully with familiar cats within the home while still being predatory around other small furry animals, or chasing unfamiliar cats outside the home. So long as you are confident that the dog is not going to practice predatory behaviours with the cat in the home, they can be left alone together, with suitable safe spaces available to both. It is also important to mention that if the dog has shown resource guarding, you should go and seek a behaviourist for further advice, and high value reinforcers may be required throughout the introduction.

4.2 Environment

The environment should be prepared so that the welfare of both the cat and the dog is upheld to reduce the impact of the change. During this stage there should be no interactions between the cat and dog, and be sure to minimise stressors in the environment. This may be more challenging if introducing puppies and kittens, who are inquisitive by nature and may seek each other out. It is important not to rush ahead with introductions and to take each stage slowly and carefully to ensure maximum success. This applies even if the cat initiates contact. Though this is a positive sign and should not be discouraged, progressing forward too quickly for either of them may impact success later down the line.

The environmental setup will be different depending on whether the cat is moving into an environment where a dog currently resides or a dog is moving into a home where a cat currently resides.

A pheromone diffuser can be used within the environment, for both the dog and the cat, before and during exposures, to provide a calming influence on them both. These artificial pheromones are used to reduce stress and anxiety, and plug-ins can be used in the individuals' safe spaces or in areas where they are likely to meet. These should not be used as a 'quick fix', however, and should only be used in a complementary manner alongside the additional exercises and management techniques. There are many types of pheromone that are suitable for use in multi-species environments. The use of pheromone diffusers may be particularly useful if introducing an amber or red-rated cat.

It is important that the cat has all her resources in a safe space that she is already comfortable in, away from a dog. Cats and dogs will often find their own preferred locations, particularly during introductions, and space needs to be managed and orchestrated carefully to maximise success. A lack of safe space and resources are key causes of frustration, often leading to conflict and other undesirable behaviours. When first introducing a new cat to a new environment it should be done as positively and in as stress free a manner as possible. It is important for all parties to be able to access space away when they need it.

If space is an issue within the home environment and additional resources and safe spaces cannot be included, it is worth considering whether adding another individual into the household is the most suitable action at this time. If they do not settle in the space, consider using a pheromonal diffuser for longer and/or give more time for them to settle, increasing pleasant interactions and use of high value rewards.

A new cat

If you are bringing a new cat into the home, then you should set up the environment with the required resources as described in Chapter 1, 1.3 Welfare Considerations. This section will provide guidance as to which resources are required, as well as information on their placement when settling a cat into a home.

Develop a safe space within her area, details of which are described in Chapter 2, Exercise 3. The resources for the new cat should be provided in her safe space when this is being set up, and should mostly include resources with her own scent on where possible. This is where it is useful to swap items between households or from the rescue centre, to try and build a scent profile in her new home. The space should be created somewhere the dog cannot access or see, and should be calm and safe. There should be no ability for the dog to scratch and paw at a door leading to her safe space or where he is able to bark and whine in close proximity. If this is going to be an issue it's worth exploring the use of more permanent barriers at a greater distance from her safe space by using safety gates.

For the new cat it is important to keep the dog out of

her space prior to her coming home, and ideally avoid them seeing each other for the first few days, at least. This will allow the new cat to build positive associations within this space and establish it as safe, as well as allow her to settle into her new environment away from additional stressors.

For dogs already in the home, their routine should not be impacted too greatly, so as not to create a negative association with the changes and the new feline addition. The cat's safe space should not be accessible to him, but he should keep his own resting and sleeping areas, away from high traffic areas, allowing him to relax too.

If the cat's safe space is somewhere that does have general household traffic, and you notice the cat isn't eating or toileting sufficiently, it may be worth placing food higher up and ensuring litter trays are out of sight as far as reasonably possible. Cats feel safer at height and when secluded and have privacy, particularly when there are other cats, dogs and/or children around.

A new dog

When bringing a new dog into a cat's home, they, too, require a safe space to be set up. This should also be somewhere away from the cat's safe space, with a quiet resting area as well as easy access to food and water. Safety gates can be used to limit access to certain areas of the house which are off limits, but he should be allowed from the outset to go everywhere that will be accessible to him. This may include the cat's feeding station, sleeping area and toileting area, just not her safe space.

If the cat is already residing within the home and the dog is coming into the environment, then her environment should stay as similar as possible, and her access should not

EXERCISES	GREEN	AMBER	RED
Exercise 7: Settle on a bed *Particularly useful for dogs that are likely to become easily aroused or excited.*	✔	✔	✔
Exercise 8: Focus on me *Particularly useful for dogs that are likely to become easily frustrated and are likely to start barking at the cat.*	✘	✔	✔
Exercise 9: Recall *Particularly useful for dogs that are likely to chase or lunge at the cat.*	✘	✘	✔
Exercise 10: Give and take *Particularly useful for dogs that can become easily frustrated.*	✘	✘	✔

Figure 4.5. The ticks ✔ identify which training exercises should be completed for dogs who scored red, amber or green. The crosses ✘ indicate exercises that are not essential, but could be useful based on each individuals' requirements; for example, if the dog becomes easily frustrated then it may be beneficial to perform the 'give and take' exercise.

be restricted. It is, however, important to make sure the cat has her safe space that the dog cannot access.

You do not need to change too much of the cat's setup or routine, and you should disrupt her space as little as possible. The dog's safe space should be somewhere that doesn't infringe on an area she prefers. Where this is not possible, make sure you create an alternate safe space for her as well, which she can become accustomed to, prior to his coming home.

4.3 Learning

Scent swapping is not required in any formal capacity as they have likely already picked up on each other's scent. However, you can swap some toys or blankets – just make sure that when you do this you also feed them, provide attention or encourage play. It is important during this time to build the cat's confidence in her environment, and prior to introducing her to the dog. Regardless of whether the dog is already there or new, there are some things you can do that will improve the chances of success when meeting the cat. Training should be undertaken prior to introducing the dog to the cat, and based on the dog's score from the canine assessment (red, amber, or green). You should use Figure 4.5 to see which training exercises would be the most useful to focus on.

From these training exercises it is important to get the dog to practise making good choices, providing clear feedback to him via the use of reinforcers. Reinforcers increase an individual's confidence and likelihood to perform desirable behaviours, and are anything the individual perceives as pleasant, such as attention, food treats, and enjoyable activities such as playing. During training, you may use quite a few treats, therefore make sure you manage the dog and cat's diet as required, for example reducing their main meals when you have provided higher volumes of food treats. You can use their dinner as well if this is enticing enough, but try to use a variety of reinforcers throughout the training and introduction. Make sure that you also provide enough toilet breaks throughout training and keep training sessions short.

Teaching a settle

A settle is important for all dogs that are being introduced to a cat, as it encourages them to be calm and understand that positive things come from being calm. This behaviour would involve the dog being encouraged to lie down on a bed and remaining settled and calm, ideally choosing to stay there. During this process he would intermittently be provided with reinforcers, such as food treats. This behaviour, settle on the bed, will be encouraged when the dog is first introduced to the cat.

Exercise 7: Settle on a bed

- Before beginning this exercise ensure your dog will have had a walk or game to expend excess energy.
- Place your dog's bed in a location where the cat and dog will first meet at a distance, ideally near the new cat's safe space but in a large enough location so that the cat does not feel trapped and can freely get back to her safe space. If the dog is new, then keep the cat away as much as possible during training to reduce the distractions, possibly by working in a separate area. Ideally start with the dog on a lead as this will be a requirement during the introduction. The lead should be loose, however, and not used to keep the dog on the bed.
- Encourage your dog over to the bed with food treats, scattering a few onto the bed. Once he is on the bed you should encourage him into a sit or a lie-down position, either using a cue that he already knows or by luring him with the food in your hand. You can lure him into a sit by lifting the food treat above his nose and over his head, or into a lying-down position by moving the food treat down from his nose onto the bed between his front paws and moving it slightly

forward. As soon as he is in either of these positions, provide him with a food treat. Alternatively, you can just continue to drop treats onto the bed and wait for him to sit or lie down himself.

- Continue feeding treats while the dog is on the bed. If the dog chooses to get off that's fine, and you can drop the lead and let him wander around for a bit. As soon as he chooses to go back onto the bed you can continue providing food, or alternatively you can actively lure him back on again, reinforcing calm and relaxed behaviours. You will have to drop regular treats initially to encourage him to stay on the bed, but, as the dog stays longer, you can reduce the treats provided and increase the time between dropping, to encourage a longer calm and relaxed settled period. Make sure you are always praising the dog. You can also use a stuffed Kong or a tasty chew to keep him occupied on his bed.

TOP TIPS

- For dogs that become easily aroused or very excited it may be harder for them to settle, so keep the sessions short to begin with and make sure you end the training sessions on a positive.
- If the dog stands up or moves off the bed, then just gently lure him back to the bed with food treats, and provide lots of attention and treats while he is lying down, slowly building the duration between food treats once the dog is fully relaxed (ideally leaning to one side).

Teaching a focus

Teaching a focus is particularly important for dogs that have scored amber or red, especially where they may become excited or frustrated easily. The aim of this exercise would be to avoid the dog getting overly aroused in the cat's presence. While settled on a bed, if he looks across at her you can request him to look back at you, breaking his attention away from her before arousal gets too high in her presence. This provides him with additional guidance and an alternative behaviour to perform that distracts him before his arousal builds too quickly and leads into an undesirable interaction.

Exercise 8: Focus on me

- The dog can be off lead during this exercise, though to begin with there should be minimal distractions in the area.
- While the dog is settled, either lying down or sitting down, grab a food reward and lure his gaze towards your face. As soon as he looks towards your face say 'good' and provide a food treat.
- Do this repeatedly until you can predict that he will follow the lure predictably. Then start to add the cue word, for example 'look', just before you lure the behaviour. You should continue to provide a food treat every time.
- Once he begins looking at you immediately after the cue you can start to phase out the lure until the dog is looking at you only on the cue.

Top tips

- As with other exercises it is important to find which rewards are reinforcing to him to ensure he is motivated to complete the exercise.

Teaching a recall

A recall is useful as a safety cue for all dogs, but is particularly important for dogs who have scored red. If the dog already has an effective recall, this will be very helpful, enabling you to call a dog away from the cat when necessary. The aim of this exercise is to build an association between a cue word and a food treat so that when the dog hears the cue word, he comes over to you from his desire for the food treat. This needs to be repeated many times for the cue word to be reliably associated with food and to encourage a habitual response in the dog to come back to you immediately. It is important to understand that a recall may not be effective if the dog really wants to chase a cat, and for this reason if he is driven by a predatory response, introducing him to a cat might not be the best course of action and should be avoided if possible.

Exercise 9: Recall

- Decide on a cue, for example the word 'here'.

- Pair the cue word with food multiple times by saying the word immediately followed by the provision of a food treat. He does not need to be performing a specific behaviour during this time, but should not be performing any undesirable behaviour. *Do not offer the food reward if undesirable behaviour takes place, wait until the behaviour ceases or offer the cue word again.*

- Do this continuously until he starts coming back to you upon presentation of the cue, in anticipation of the food being provided. You should then also reinforce this response and continue to practice this in more distracting environments.

Top tips

- Make sure you are in a quiet and non-distracting environment so that the cue is clearly audible to the dog, which will help when building the association.

- The dog does not have to come to you during the initial training, as to start with you are focusing on building an association between the cue and food. So, as long as the two are presented in close proximity to each other while the dog is not distracted, he should learn that the cue means food is coming.

- Leave a short gap between each presentation to allow the dog to eat the food treat, for example: cue, food, short pause, cue, food, short pause, etc.

Teaching to swap

The aim of this exercise is to teach the dog to release a toy or chew that he currently has possession of, upon request. This will be useful for dogs that have scored red, as it can build the dog's tolerance to frustration, and teaching him that giving up a resource can result in gaining more valuable resources, which could assist in reducing arousal and frustration.. This exercise should not be undertaken if the dog already shows resource guarding, and you should seek professional behavioural help for this first, as it will require more in-depth support.

Exercise 10: Give and take

- Gather a range of high and low value food treats and then provide your dog with one of his favourite toys.
- Encourage a game and once he is engaged in the game and has hold of the toy offer him a high value food treat (holding it close to his nose so that he can smell it).
- As soon as he lets go of the toy give him the treat. After he has eaten the treat you can begin the game again. If he is reluctant to release the toy, then hold the toy still and offer a higher value treat or a higher value toy to swap with instead (if he is more toy motivated).
- Once he is consistently and predictably releasing the toy on presentation of a treat, you can begin to add in the verbal cue (eg, 'drop') JUST BEFORE you present the treat, so that he is listening to the cue and is not distracted by the treat. Continue to practise this on a regular basis.

Top tips

- If he gets too aroused during play, it's best to distract him with an alternative activity such as going outside, or another training exercise such as 'settle on a bed'.

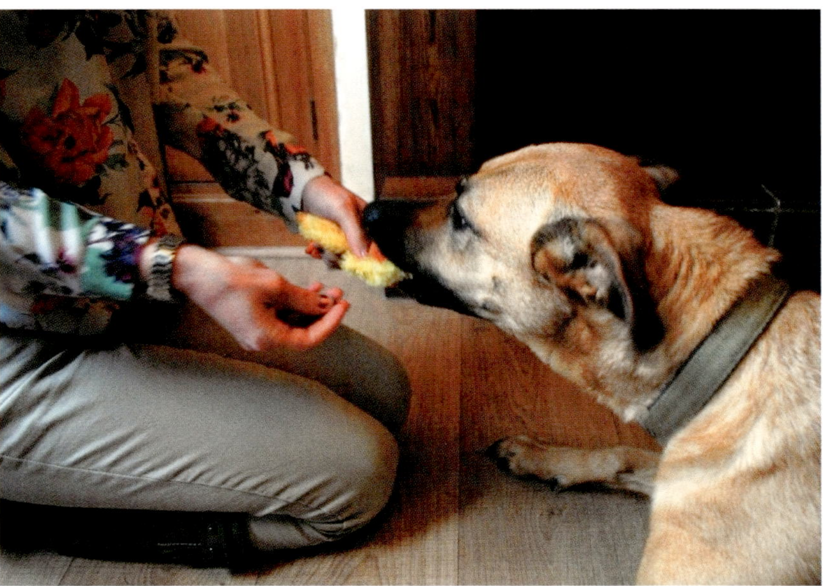

Hold one end of the toy in one hand while presenting a treat in the other and then give him the treat when he lets go of the toy.

4.4 Interactions

For both the cat and dog, the aims throughout the introductions are to focus on encouraging appropriate behaviours and to build confidence. In addition to this, the priority for the cat during the introductions is for her to investigate and scent mark the space, while not feeling threatened by the dog. The priority for the dog is for him to be encouraged to make the right choices while in the presence of the cat, by remaining calm and relaxed throughout the interactions. This should be done by setting up the environment for them both to succeed, and by reinforcing desirable behaviours while also preventing arousal and undesirable behaviours such as barking, lunging or chasing.

Preparing for the introduction

Prior to introductions you should take the dog for a walk or play with him to allow him to burn off some energy. To set up the environment to succeed, have the dog's bed furthest away from where the cat will enter the space. The location should be quite a large space where the cat can move through while maintaining a distance from the dog. The first introductions should be controlled, with the dog placed on a lead as a precaution rather than an active restraint. The lead should ideally not have to be used to hold back the dog, and instead the dog should be encouraged to remain relaxed on the bed. Provide a tasty chew or filled Kong that will keep him entertained while he is laid on his bed. You should also have plenty of high value food treats for both the dog and the cat. Ideally you should have two people, one who will hold the end of the lead and focus on reinforcing the dog in the settle, while the other is available to provide feedback to the cat. If there is only you, focus on the dog by holding the lead and engaging with them, encouraging appropriate responses while the cat explores. You should only do this when you are sure you can manage the dog's arousal, and need to be very observant of the cat getting too close and causing the dog to get too excited.

Tails entwined: a guide to cat-dog introductions

If the dog has not had previous experience living with or being around cats before, you need to be extra careful during these first introductions, making sure these are done slowly and with lots of positive reinforcement for calm behaviour. Younger dogs are likely to be less experienced and more excitable, which can also lead to increased arousal, an increased likelihood of frustration, and inappropriate behaviours, therefore first exposures need to be managed carefully. Take the dog for a walk or have a play session beforehand, so that he has a bit less energy, particularly if he is a younger dog. During the introductions provide lots of reinforcement, both to the dog for making correct choices, and to the cat to build her confidence.

Use Exercise 11 for the introduction, and avoid undesirable behaviours from the dog such as chasing or barking at the cat, as well as avoiding either of them getting too aroused or excited. Techniques to help manage the cat's arousal have been described in Figure 2.9 of Chapter 2, and techniques to help manage the dog's arousal are described in Figure 4.3 within this chapter. In addition, there is further troubleshooting advice provided in Figure 4.6.

If there are more than two individuals being introduced to each other, you'll need multiple people to help provide food treats and attention to all individuals. Make sure you take introductions slower; put in the groundwork first and continually observe all the individuals' behaviours carefully. Follow the advice below for multiple introductions:

- For multiple cats and a dog, ensure you have a variety of high value food treats and more distractions for the dog, and follow the same process to introduce them, letting each cat approach in their own time.
- For multiple dogs and a cat, introduce each dog separately to the cat, particularly if there is one individual that is more excitable or more likely to become aroused. Follow the same process to introduce them, introducing the dog with the best score first (ie, green before amber or red, and amber before red). This will allow the cat to build their confidence around a polite dog first. If most or all the dogs have scored green, the separate introductions to the cat may not be necessary, but make sure you can manage the environment appropriately.
- If there are multiple cats as well as dogs, keep the cats together during the introduction. However, if you have an easily aroused cat, it may be beneficial to delay introductions for this individual until after the others have met, enabling you to focus your attention on keeping arousal levels low for more positive introductions.

Exercise 11: Introducing cats and dogs

- Open all the doors inside the house to allow the cat to enter the location where the dog is. Allow her to enter the location in her own time, or you can encourage her into the space if the dog is settled and lying on his bed, as previously trained. In these early exposures it is important to continuously reinforce the dog with high value food treats, to make being settled on the bed and focused on you more valuable than approaching the cat.

- Allow the cat to choose the distance between herself and the dog, so all interactions are led by her. It is important to avoid chase behaviour and therefore his behaviour must be carefully observed for an increase in arousal due to a barrier or sight of the cat, who he can't get to. He may become fearful or aroused if he wants to greet or chase the cat, and he cannot. She may also become fearful or aroused if she cannot get away from him, and will also need some encouragement at this time.

- Let her explore in her own time. Try not to smother her while she is investigating, however encourage positive emotional states and confidence by providing her with attention, by stroking or brushing her, or high value food treats. Follow her lead with regards to what constitutes enticing a positive emotional state. Be aware that she may not take the food treats initially, or want any attention, as she will be getting a feel for her surroundings and may just want to explore. You can also encourage her to go up onto surfaces to feel safer while she is scent marking via facial rubbing, but let it be her choice where she explores.

- Always keep both individuals under the threshold for stress by reinforcing good decisions and calm responses. Either party may get excited, especially him, but only let them sniff one another at this stage, luring him back to you and reinforcing. It is important not to let him bark or paw at her, or lunge and chase her. He should be kept on a lead and provided with distractions such as chews and reinforcements while in her presence, using some of the training activities suggested in this chapter.

The cat should be the one to approach the dog, who should be settled and calm. They should both be as relaxed as possible.

The aim is to get the cat and dog to a point where they can relax while in the same environment as each other and be able to perform a range of natural behaviours such as grooming. They do not necessarily need to be in close proximity, however the distance that they maintain from each other is likely to reduce over time.

- Throughout the exercise it is important to keep the dog in a settle. He should be free to look across at the cat, you can tell him he is good in a calm voice, and then get him to refocus on you, while you continue to provide him with reinforcers, such as attention and high value food treats, for remaining calm.

- Let the cat approach the dog. However, try to avoid the dog approaching the cat. If the cat approaches the dog, allow the dog to lean forward and sniff but refocus his attention back onto yourself soon afterwards, as previously trained. Make sure you continue to provide lots of reinforcement for calm responses and avoid the dog standing up or moving too fast, especially if he is a large dog, as this may spook the cat. The cat should be in control of the distance, but both should be made to feel as comfortable as possible. If the dog is uncomfortable or getting too aroused by how close the cat is getting, calmly increase the distance or provide higher value food treats. Build up the distance to where he can look at her while staying seated or choosing to sit and/or look back at you. You may need to use continuous reinforcement (continually feeding him), particularly as she gets closer.

  She is likely to keep a distance, however if she approaches keep an eye on both of their responses. Avoid any negative interactions and actively try and distract the more confident individual if you feel one is struggling and showing signs of nervousness. If possible, avoid it getting to the point where the cat needs to hiss, but if she does then just distract her, increase the distance between them, and reinforce her. Equally, if the dog is too aroused to take the food treats and cannot be distracted by toys, you may need to increase the distance or stop the introduction and go back a stage (to 4.3 Learning), and do further training with him before reintroducing.

- Continue to reinforce appropriate calm responses, and the cat will usually decide when she wants to move away or back into her safe space, at which point the dog can then be taken off lead. These sessions should be kept short at first and end on a positive. You should do a few of these sessions before progressing, however if she has settled somewhere high up or she is relaxed, and he does not show much interest in her, you can continue.

- Once they are both mostly settled in each other's presence and their behaviours around each other are more predictable, such as him choosing to settle and remain calm on a loose lead, then you can remove the lead. When doing this make sure there are lots of distractions in the environment, such as toys and food treats, but make sure the environment remains calm. Continue engaging with him by doing training or providing attention or giving him a chew. Ideally have at least two people, someone to engage with each individual, and continue to monitor behaviour.

- There should be a natural transition with the cat choosing to spend more time around the dog, decreasing the distance between each other and performing more active behaviours in his presence, such as playing or scratching on a scratch post.

- Only leave them alone together when you can trust there will not be conflict between them, and they have been relaxed in each other's presence. Ensure both individuals still have access to a safe space, with hers ideally being at height, so they can escape if required.

Top tips

- Feeding them their dinner in view of each other but at a distance or, ideally, where she is high up can also build confidence, however if they won't eat you should continue to feed them separately or in their safe spaces.
- If she engages in positively reinforcing behaviours such as playing or eating, then this will also help increase her confidence.
- Avoid loud noises, and quick or sudden movements in these early stages as she is likely to be already cautious while exploring. Note: Whenever they are in each other's presence, make sure the environment stays calm and that you provide plenty of reinforcement in the form of nice food treats or attention/stroking (as long as this is something they enjoy). Promote appropriate responses by stroking/feeding them both while they stay calm and show confidence. Try to avoid negative interaction, and go back a stage if you feel either is struggling, looking panicked, nervous or particularly aroused.
- They may just tolerate each other, and they may prefer to keep their distance from each other. There may be a bit of hissing or spitting from her if he gets too close, but so long as nothing escalates, just continue to keep everything positive, and keep providing reinforcement.
- While he is on lead you should continue to watch for signs of agitation or arousal, as frustration could be building.
- It is okay to allow the cat to go outside, if she already does this, but avoid her fleeing outside to get away from him, as she may then be too nervous to come back in the house. Also make sure she has access to her safe space from the outside without having to engage with him.
- You may want to use the highest value food treats for close interactions to ensure maximum reinforcement.
- Avoid allowing any chasing of each other, unless it is obvious play behaviour. However, true play is unlikely to happen between unfamiliar individuals straight away.
- She should always have the space so that if she wants to move away or go back into her safe space, increasing the distance between her and him, she can.
- Do not begin this when either of them is particularly hungry as they may become more easily frustrated in each other's presence.
- Providing the high value food treats only on these occasions may also speed up the process of making the association between the sight of each other and the treats, and therefore learn more quickly that neither are a threat.

4.5 Dynamics

It is important to continuously monitor the ongoing interactions and welfare of both the cat and the dog. It may be normal for the occasional hiss or chase, but where you feel that the she is continually or acutely stressed, is hiding a lot more, or is suppressing her natural behaviours, then you should consider how her welfare can be improved. This could be by adjusting the environment by introducing more vertical space to make her feel safer, creating more barriers or building her confidence. Furthermore, if the dog is continually over-aroused, cannot settle in her presence, wants to chase and becomes fixated easily on her, then further training is required. It is important to continue using positive reinforcement for desirable behaviours and to promote harmonious interactions; however, it may be necessary to go back a stage and consult the troubleshooting advice (Figure 4.6) for further guidance.

Issues	Action
Avoidance	Increase the distance and build the cat's confidence while she can see the dog, but the dog can't see her, building it up to where he can see her. If you have a dog who scored green and keeps his distance, then you can still allow her to access all areas while building her confidence. Provide more vertical spaces in the environment and encourage the cat to go higher where she will be more comfortable taking food in the dogs presence, and they can manage their distance better. Continue providing reinforcement to maintain calm behaviours and encourage positive emotional states.
Chase	If either attempt to chase, stop it immediately and provide the animal who was chased with reassurance and some attention/reinforcement to reduce the stress. You should increase the distance between them and use high value reinforcers to encourage calm behaviours. Do not punish the chase behaviour, just make sure you set up the environment to avoid this in future. If a dog chases a cat it can be detrimental to building the cat's confidence. On occasions a dog may chase a familiar cat during play, however, unless this is a reciprocal interaction that the cat actively encourages it should be discouraged wherever possible. This should be done by refocusing the dog's excitement or play onto something more appropriate. If the chase is more predatory you should end the interaction, separate the individuals, and reconsider their suitability to be housed together.
Fixation or staring	Redirect the attention of both individuals, ideally using higher value reinforcers, while increasing the distance between them. End the interaction if either becomes very tense as though they are going to launch. Go back a stage and give them more time. Do extra training with them and find alternative reinforcers that may be higher value.
Excessive play or inappropriate play	Redirect their play towards toys, and provide them with a range of alternative enrichment to keep them occupied and reduce their energy. While playing, keep them separate from the cat while they expel their energy. Encourage calm behaviours around the other animal by doing some extra training. Provide reinforcement to both the cat and dog for making right choices.

Figure 4.6. General troubleshooting, identifying some behaviour that may occur during interactions and how to deal with them.

If it is difficult to manage interactions due to inappropriate play or agonistic behaviours, you should consider the welfare of both the cat and the dog in this scenario, especially if you have tried the troubleshooting activities, taken your time throughout the process, or the environment cannot be adjusted significantly to allow for better progression. If during any of this process, you are concerned for either individuals' welfare or behaviour, or you see very little progression in being able to integrate them safely, first go to a vet to check their health, in case there is any underlying cause. Alternatively, you can get back in touch with the place where you obtained the new cat or dog for advice, or contact an accredited behaviourist for further specialist support.

Cats and dogs can build harmonious relationships.

5: Cats and kids

This chapter focuses on introducing cats to children, and for ease of reading children will be referred to as they/them. Children are a significant part of many homes, either as residents or visitors, so it's important to prepare both the children and the cats to be around each other. It is also advisable to prepare a cat to be around children when a family are expecting to have a baby or child join the family. Cats who are joining a family also need to be assessed for their suitability to living in a home with children. This chapter will cover:

- Assessing the likelihood of whether a cat can successfully live with children
- The best way to prepare the individuals for meeting to improve the likelihood of a successful and harmonious interactions
- How to introduce them for the best success
- How to monitor and manage ongoing interactions and troubleshoot potential issues, including how to improve current relationships

A relationship between a child and a cat can be very beneficial for both individuals. Children are likely to spend time playing with cats, enriching both their lives, while a cat can also provide companionship for them. Children can also learn a great deal about responsibility, relationships and grief. It is essential that their relationships and interactions are harmonious however, and that appropriate play sessions are encouraged. This is because cat bites and scratches can have serious health effects, and should therefore be avoided where possible. This is one of the reasons teaching both cats and children appropriate play techniques is important, to prevent the use of teeth and claws during interactions with people.

Cats and children can benefit from living together.

Cats that have previously lived with or been around children are more likely to have been exposed to the range of noises and movements that children make, and are therefore more likely to accept living with them. This does not mean, however, that inexperienced cats will not be able to accept living with children, but they may just require more time to adjust, depending on the ages of the children. The individuals, their experiences, their personality

Stage	Exercise	Measure of success	Record of progress
Upon meeting success at each stage you can progress to the next stage, however if there are any difficulties at each stage look at troubleshooting and/or move back a stage.			*Example: the children have demonstrated an understanding about how to interact safely with cats.*
Stage one: Create safe spaces	3 (and 2)	The cat is relaxed and carrying out a range of natural behaviours in their spaces, such as grooming, playing, resting.	
Stage two: Educate the children	Young children	The children have engaged in discussions about cat behaviour and the DO's and DON'T's when interacting with cats	
	Older children	As with young children but can also identify ways of managing arousal.	
Stage three: Introduction	12	The cat is mostly relaxed and is performing natural behaviours in the children's presence. There is no fear shown and they are both behaving appropriately towards each other.	

Figure 5.1. The process to follow when introducing a cat to children.

and behavioural traits need to be considered prior to introductions, and children should be educated about cat behaviour and how to behave around cats. Figure 5.1 demonstrates the process to follow to introduce a cat to a child or children in the most successful manner. You can use this as a record of your progress. If you struggle to progress at any stage you should refer to the guidance throughout this chapter.

5.1 Feline friends

When introducing cats to children the main aim is to reduce and prevent fear in the cat when around children, and therefore focus on building her confidence. It is also important to maintain safety, and therefore, as well as managing the cat's arousal, it is important to consider the age of the child, as this will influence how they respond to her.

You should have already completed Feline Assessment 3, from Chapter 2, Figure 2.12, regarding your cat. Remember that if your cat is a true feral under two months old or a non-feral under four months old, then the cat can be instantly scored as green. Otherwise you should have completed the assessment. This will have provided you with a score of red, amber, or green for her which, along with the age of the child, will guide your approach, as identified in Figure 5.2.

The cat's score and the child's age allow us to make predictions on the likely success of the introduction and what adjustments might help improve the chances of success. Guidance is provided on how the environment and the individuals can be prepared prior to the introduction, as summarised in Figure 5.3.

When you are setting up the environment and introducing the individuals you should be mindful of what caused the cat to score how she did, for instance if she had shown avoidance behaviour during past interactions around children, or if she does not adapt well to new situations. To reduce the likelihood of her becoming stressed, you might want to start by doing more confidence building (Chapter 3 Exercise 2).

If you have not yet chosen your new cat, you should seek advice from her previous home, for example the rescue centre or breeder, who would have assessed the likely sociability of the cats within their care. You may also wish to share the exercise with them to help support the scoring.

If you are introducing multiple cats then you should complete Feline Assessment 3 (Chapter 2) for each cat and follow the guidance for those that have the worst scores. If you are introducing multiple children then follow the guidance based on the age of the youngest child, as shown in Figure 5.2.

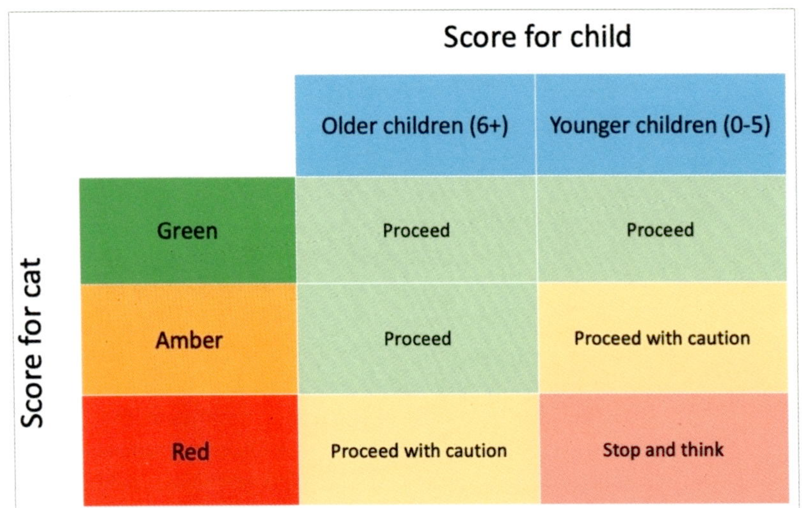

Score for cat	Score for child: Older children (6+)	Score for child: Younger children (0-5)
Green	Proceed	Proceed
Amber	Proceed	Proceed with caution
Red	Proceed with caution	Stop and think

Figure 5.2. Using the scores for both the cat and the age of the youngest child you can see which approach you should take prior to introducing them together.

Note:

The ages of the children have been split into 0-5 and 6+ years of age based on general traits such as energy levels, level of patience, focus, noise, and ability to remain calm and have gentle hands. These can be flexible, and if your child is neurodiverse, they may not sit within the suggested age ranges based on behaviour. It is important to use your own discretion, considering an individual child's behaviour, personality traits, and their level of experience with cats or other animals. For example, if they have had a positive experience with cats before, know how to behave around cats so as not to scare them, and/or have strong listening and remaining calm traits, then they will adjust well around cats. Those individuals who do not have such experience or traits may require more assistance. If the child in question is a baby, there are fewer issues regarding personality traits and experience, but exercises relating to younger children should be followed.

Proceed: Where you're introducing a cat with a green rating to children of any age, or an amber-rated cat with older children, it is okay to proceed with the introduction process as described in this chapter. Smooth and successful interactions are never guaranteed, but success is more likely in these scenarios. Because kittens are more likely to scratch and bite hands during play it is important to take care when they are around children, and it's therefore key to manage the cat's arousal. All children should be advised on cat behaviour and appropriate interactions. It may also be useful to prepare cats for new noises that are associated with younger children and babies if they have not experienced children of these ages before. Guidance on this can be found within this chapter.

Proceed with caution: Where a cat with an amber rating is being introduced to younger children, or a red-rated cat to older children, you should proceed with caution. The time needed will vary depending on individual personalities: you should monitor behaviours and responses sufficiently, and only move to the next stage once you are comfortable the cat and children are ready. Space, perseverance and management will be key factors in ensuring a successful introduction, and ultimately, relationship between the cat and the child(ren). It may be worthwhile considering here that your cat and child(ren) may never have a positive relationship with many interactions, and expectations need to be set regarding this. So long as there are no welfare implications for the cat, and no safety concerns for the children, it is possible for an amber-rated cat to live quite contently within her own space, being unbothered by children.

Stop and think: Where the cat has scored red and you want to introduce her to younger children, then you should stop and think, considering if the cat is going to settle in the children's presence, and/or if she poses a risk to the children. Cats who score red are likely to become easily aroused and either have scratched and bitten in the past, or are highly likely to. This may be due to a negative emotional state; however, it could also be due to undesirable play such as grabbing hands, or excess energy that is not redirected effectively. Managing arousal is therefore very important. This is particularly important if the cat already resides in the household, because if she does not adapt well to new situations, is unpredictable or quickly aroused, this may cause her to scratch or swipe the child.

Your cat should feel safe and secure within her home as this provides her with the foundation to be receptive to change and adapt accordingly. If the cat is new to the household, then it may be important to consider whether

<table>
<tr><th></th><th></th><th colspan="2">CHILDREN</th><th colspan="4">CATS</th></tr>
<tr><th></th><th>Cat's score</th><th>Educate older children</th><th>Educate younger children</th><th>Create a safe space (Exercise 3)</th><th>Build cat's confidence (Exercise 2)</th><th>Prevent and manage arousal</th><th>Use a pheromonal diffuser</th></tr>
<tr><td rowspan="2">Proceed</td><td>Green</td><td rowspan="2">✔</td><td>✔</td><td rowspan="2">✔</td><td rowspan="2">✗</td><td rowspan="2">✗</td><td rowspan="2">✗</td></tr>
<tr><td>Amber</td><td></td></tr>
<tr><td rowspan="2">Proceed with caution</td><td>Amber</td><td></td><td>✔</td><td>✔</td><td>✔</td><td>✗</td><td rowspan="2">✗</td></tr>
<tr><td>Red</td><td>✔</td><td></td><td>✔✔</td><td>✔</td><td>✔</td></tr>
<tr><td>Stop and think</td><td>Red</td><td></td><td>✔✔</td><td>✔✔</td><td>✔✔</td><td>✔</td><td>✔</td></tr>
</table>

Figure 5.3. This figure provides a summary of what should be carried out with the children and cats based on whether your results indicated 'Proceed', 'Proceed with caution' or 'Stop and think'. Additional guidance is given based on whether the cat has scored red, amber, or green. A single tick identifies which tasks/exercises should be completed. Two ticks means that you need to spend more time doing the tasks/ exercises. The crosses indicate when you should consider the use of the tasks/exercises based on the individual child/children and cat; it could be a good idea to undertake these if the child has not been around cats before and vice versa. The grey shaded sections are irrelevant and can be ignored.

she is the right individual to introduce to the family. If the introduction is unavoidable, extra care needs to be taken when setting up a safe space and carrying out the introductions. You can improve the chances of success by taking things slowly, at the cat's pace, continually manage arousal, and understand that it may take a lot longer to see any success. Be prepared that she may never fully accept the integration, and therefore her welfare should be continuously monitored.

You should consider rehoming the cat if her welfare is negatively impacted for a prolonged period, particularly if she does not have a safe space or the environment cannot be managed to where the cat can get away from the children. This may be especially important with very young children or neurodiverse children. Her welfare is a key priority and there are times when rehoming is the best outcome for all involved. However, it is recommended to seek behaviour support from a qualified and accredited behaviourist in these situations to explore all avenues prior to rehoming. Although important for all cats, it is particularly important for red-rated cats to make sure you are avoiding situations that trigger frustration. Make sure you allow her the opportunity and space to make appropriate choices such as being able to move away, and always reinforce calm behaviours.

5.2 Environment

As established in Chapter 1, cats thrive on predictability and routine, and can often experience stress when there are sudden changes or unpredictable behaviours. For existing cats in the household, an established and consistent routine for feeding, play and human interaction is important, especially as there will be changes to an environment when a new baby or child enters it. Changes to an existing environment should be made slowly, building confidence and familiarity to new objects gradually over a period prior to introductions, as discussed in section 5.3.

Safe space

When setting up the environment it is essential to establish a safe space for the cat as well as provide all the required resources within that space, as described in Exercise 3 in Chapter 2. A safe space should be set up in the household, regardless of whether she is currently living there or is new to the environment. This should be a space where she can escape the sights and sounds of children, and a private space, at least until she is more relaxed around the children. The safe space should be as free from noise as possible, particularly during the settling in period.

Safety considerations

When considering the cat's wider environment consider the use of vertical space, as this can provide her with confidence and allow her additional options to access space away from young children when she wants to eat or rest. Providing a range of enrichment is also likely to reduce her likelihood of becoming frustrated, and direct any excitement or energy to appropriate resources and toys; this helps manage arousal. An important consideration will be the location for latrine spaces, which should be inaccessible to children for safety and hygiene reasons, particularly for younger children. Feeding areas should also be inaccessible to children, from a hygiene perspective, but also to enable a secure area for her to feed, without fear or distress. Cats are very cautious when feeding, many preferring shallow bowls so they can see clearly around them throughout. Compromises to the feeding area may mean she is reluctant to feed, and could impact her behaviour and welfare in the long term.

For any areas that will be off-limits to a cat upon a baby's arrival, it is important to gradually reduce her time in these spaces. You can do this by reducing the size of the space as well as the amount of time she is allowed in it, over several weeks. By doing this gradually she will not become distressed by a sudden change and will allow for a sense of adaptability, which can improve relations when baby arrives.

Areas such as pushchairs, Moses baskets, bassinets, cots or beds should remain off bounds where possible to prevent any potential negative interactions and safety issues. Where babies need to sleep in the same room as an adult, which could be an area the cat has access to, especially in the day, safety nets can be used to discourage access.

The nets should discourage her from jumping into the space, keeping the sleeping areas hygienic, and preventing undesirable contact between her and the baby, especially when unsupervised. It is also worth making sure you can separate the cat and child without impacting welfare during times when you are not able to engage in active supervision. This can be done by providing the cat with alternative entertainment or treats during these times, activity feeders are useful tools at this time as they engage her in play, but also provide food which will maintain her focus.

If you are pregnant, you should also ideally not be emptying cat litter trays and should get another member of the household to do this for you, due to the risk of toxoplasmosis. If this is unavoidable, wear gloves, wash hands thoroughly and maintain good personal hygiene.

5.3 Learning

Prior to introductions, spend time building the cat's confidence, particularly if she has never been around children before (using Exercise 2); this can be done while she is in her safe space or in her current environment. Feeding the cat while she can see the children at a distance can be useful for building her confidence around them. This is particularly important if she has scored amber or red, or if she is being introduced to a baby or young children, who are often unpredictable in their movement and vocalisations. In these instances, you should focus on noises and moving objects that are associated with babies and/or young children and follow the steps outlined below to increase the cat's exposure to these.

Time should be spent educating children about cat behaviour and how to interact with cats safely, particularly if the children are younger or have not been around cats before. Adults and older children should also be aware of how to read arousal in cats, and be aware of how to avoid and manage arousal if it increases, as described in Chapter 2 (Figure 2.9).

Babies and cats

One of the key factors to keep in mind is that of preparation. If you have the luxury of time, then preparations are the best place to start, and can make a real difference in future introductions. This works if you are bringing a new baby into an existing cat's space, but also if you are bringing a new cat into an environment where there is already a baby present.

Babies and the unpredictable, loud noises they make can be a significant stressor for cats, and one which can impact interactions and future relationships. It is therefore a good idea to prepare cats for such noises prior to the event. There are many apps and websites available, free of charge, that simulate common baby sounds, and can be used for desensitisation. Experiment with a variety of pitches and cries, so your cat is confident regardless of the child and vocalisation. You can also carry out desensitisation using other items such as baby toys and large objects such as walkers and pushchairs. For guidance on how to carry out desensitisation, please see Chapter 2, Exercise 2: Building confidence.

Note that the stimulus will be the thing that you are wanting to build confidence with, whether that is the sound of a baby crying, interactions with a baby walker or even smells.

If you are bringing a new cat into a home with an existing baby then the above training still applies, it may just be that some of the training needs to be undertaken in the place she is being obtained from, if possible. If not, then some of the training can be done while she is in the safe space. You can also undertake scent swapping by taking used baby muslins or bibs and placing them with her, positively reinforcing calm, disinterested behaviour as well as positive interactions. The home should be set up in preparation for her arrival with her safe space and any out of bounds areas suitably blocked off, meaning she never has access to these areas.

Toddlers and toe beans

Cats can be instinctively fearful of loud and new stimuli, especially if they have not been raised around such stimuli and/or in busy environments. Babies, toddlers and young children can be very loud and tend to grab at cat's fur and tails as this is their method of investigation.

How do we know Hazel is playful?

Tail flicking from side to side

Crouching and wiggling her rear-end

Wide eyes

Upright forward-facing ears

Grasping out or pouncing at objects

Chasing movements

How do we know Hazel is happy?

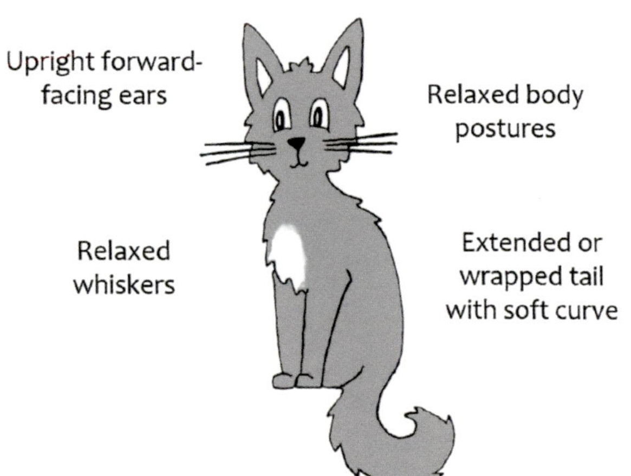

How do we know Hazel is happy?

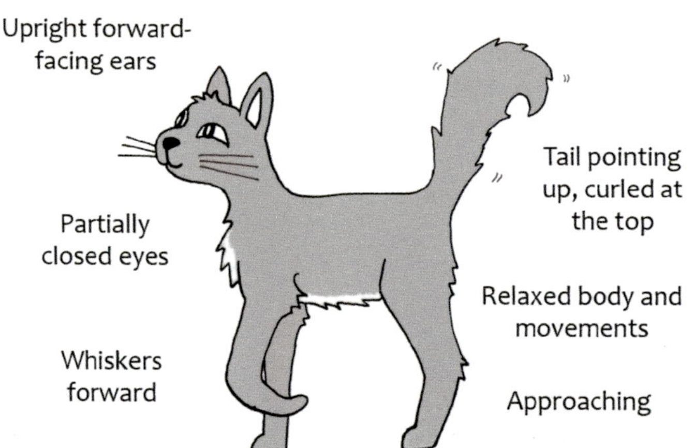

How do we know Hazel is unhappy?

How do we know Hazel is unhappy?

Ears angled backwards or sideways

Head low

Whiskers back

Tail held low down

Body tense and held low to the ground

Moving away

How do we know Hazel is unhappy?

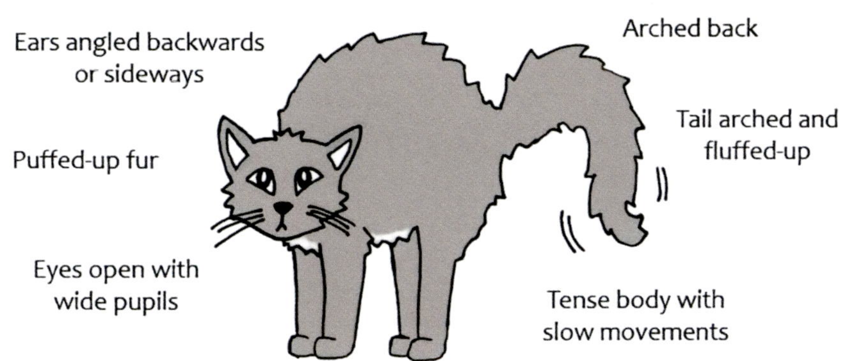

The Sociable Cat

To promote the most appropriate interactions so that your cat does not come to fear children is crucial. However, it is also important to acknowledge that it is not necessary for her to 'enjoy' or want to be around your toddler, so long as she isn't constantly fearful of them, as this will affect her contentment and welfare within the home. Therefore, along with building her confidence to various sounds and objects associated with toddlers (as previously described in the 'babies and cats' section) you should also educate your child about how to interact with the cat.

Young children, particularly toddlers, can be difficult to manage around cats, and doing so safely requires increased vigilance and patience, particularly if the cat scored red, but also being mindful of those who scored amber and the reasons behind these scores. Toddlers sometimes move quite erratically, and their behaviour can be unpredictable. They can also be quite noisy and loud, all of which can be very scary for some cats. Young children cannot read a cat's body language as easily as someone older, and scratches and bites are a frequent result of a lack of general behavioural awareness, increasing the likelihood of occurrence in children. Bites and scratches not only have the potential to cause physical damage but can also negatively affect interactions and future relationships, and should be avoided at all costs.

Advise your child of the DOs and DON'Ts of interacting with cats; these include how and when they should interact with the cat as well as when they should avoid interacting with her, as shown in Figure 5.4. This is generic advice however, and each cat will have their own preferences as to where they like to be touched. The illustrations of Hazel the cat on the previous pages should be used to instigate discussion appropriate to your children's ages and level of understanding. These can be used to discuss Hazel's behaviour and what her body postures could be indicating about how she feels. Talk about how these behaviours may influence how the child should interact with the cat, and consider different situations such as when she has initiated an interaction in a relaxed manner, when she is settled, or when she looks tense and should not be approached. Each illustration has a question and

DON'T:	DO:
• grab the cat's fur or hug the cat	• gently stroke the cat with a flat hand across the cat's back
• touch the cat's face, paws, ears, belly or tail	• groom the cat with a brush, as long as she enjoys this
• touch the cat when she is eating and/or playing	• interact with the cat when she chooses to approach
• take the cat's toys while she is playing with them	• use dangler toys such as feather wands to maintain distance
• take the cat's food while she is eating	• leave the cat alone while she is eating
• disturb or wake the cat when asleep	• engage in alternative activities such as reading to the cat
• tease the cat with food or feed from your hand	• eat away from the cat and provide treats on the floor
• feed the cat something that could make her ill	• safely offer appropriate treats when she is calm
• lift, carry, pursue or chase the cat	

Figure 5.4. The DOs and DON'Ts of how and when children should interact with cats.

A cat approaching a child for an interaction. This cat is exhibiting a greeting posture with her tail up in the air and soft and relaxed movements. The child is crouched down to be less intimidating for the cat.

some behavioural indicators that you can use to discuss with your child about how Hazel might be feeling. You can then use these illustrations alongside Figure 5.4 so that your child can understand how to interact with her based on her behaviours.

Make it clear to children about the importance of remaining calm around cats, and explain that they should always let the cat approach them rather than them approach the cat. Depending on the child's age, it is also good to discuss ending interactions on a positive note and before either party become aroused, frustrated or overwhelmed. This will need to be supervised and managed with younger children to ensure thresholds are not exceeded. It is always better to end the interaction too soon, rather than too late, to maintain positivity.

There are some excellent resources available that can be used by parents to assist in educating children about cat behaviour, some of these can be found on the websites of the following organisations:

- International Cat Care
- Cats Protection
- RSPCA 'Royal Society for the Prevention of Cruelty to Animals'
- Blue Cross

These resources help children understand how to correctly interpret cat behaviour, and how to make the right choices around cats in various everyday situations. Using these resources will enable you to help your children recognise when a cat is relaxed and comfortable with a situation, and when she is saying that she has had enough. It is essential that you always supervise these interactions and assist your child during any interactions.

5.4 Interactions

Introducing cats to children does not need to be as structured as when introducing two cats to each other or when introducing a cat to a dog. For any situation the cat's choice for space and boundaries should be respected based on her individual needs. Interact with her in the way that she

Children should be taught to stroke a cat with a flat hand across the shoulders and back instead of grabbing fur. As babies motor skills advance they may grab at fur, so you should always supervise these interactions until you can encourage more appropriate touch. It is also important for children to stay calm during these interactions.

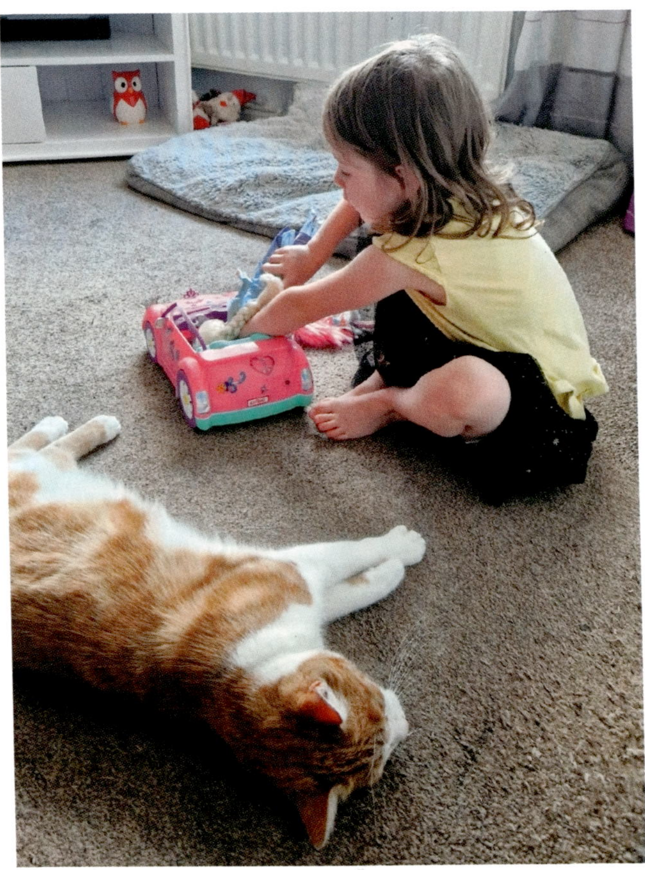

Children should be taught that while a cat is resting or sleeping, the child should engage in calm activities to avoid disturbing her.

prefers and enjoys, and always be aware of her behaviour and arousal level, particularly when she is around young children. The time it takes for the cat to settle within the same space as the children will depend on each individual, but the most important considerations during this period are:

- To keep the children calm and occupied while the cat is investigating the environment. This should continue for the period in which the cat is settling in. If possible, introduce calmer or older children to her first so she can build her confidence as well as trust.
- Not to allow the children into her safe space during initial introductions and interactions. She needs to feel confident and secure that she will be undisturbed in this area. Once this period is over, it may be useful for children of an appropriate age to feed her in this area to further build trust and positive associations.
- During the settling in period, if the children are going to engage in noisy activities, then move them into a different space where possible, particularly if the cat is quite nervous.
- Do not force an interaction and make sure the children do not approach the cat, but if she approaches them they can provide a treat, a fisted hand or gentle strokes. Try to promote a positive emotional state throughout the settling in period by providing reinforcement to her in the form of treats or attention that she likes. Allow her to move away if she chooses, and make sure she is not followed or chased.

When the cat can perform a range of natural behaviours such as grooming, resting and eating in the same area as the child/children then this shows the cat is now confident around them.

It is important for children to understand that each cat is different and that they may need to alter how they interact with each individual.

- To make sure you manage the cat's arousal level throughout, or if she is playful, encourage appropriate play using dangling toys. Continue to observe her arousal levels, and if it is building in a negative manner, or she is becoming too feisty in her play, then either change the interactions for calmer ones by scattering some food treats onto the floor away from you or stop the interaction safely. See Figure 2.9 for further ideas on managing arousal.

Only once the cat chooses to settle in the same space as the children and exhibits a range of natural behaviours such as grooming and/or playing, then the children can increase their activities while in the same space. There are a range of activities that can be encouraged if children want to interact with the cat, with examples given in Figure 5.5. Where children are interacting with the cat, particularly when stroking her, they should stop the activity after a short while to make sure she still wants to engage in the interaction, this will be indicated by the cat looking towards the child and possibly moving towards them.

Some cats can be very resilient and patient around children, and some enjoy the interactions and actively seek these out, whereas others only like certain types of interactions at their own discretion. These individual differences should be discussed with children, particularly where you see changes in your cat's behaviour or preferences due to health and age, or where there are multiple cats within the home with differing personalities. Figure 5.5

		CHILDREN				CATS		
		Younger	Older	Nervous around cats	Neurodiverse	Nervous	Confident	Easily frustrated or aroused
Relaxing	Direct contact eg stroking	*	✔	*	*	**	✔	✔
	Indirect contact eg reading or drawing	✔	✔	✔	✔	✔	✔	✔
	Brushing	*	✔	*	*	**	✔	***
Feeding and enrichment	Feeding dinner	✔	✔	✔	✔	✔	✔	✔
	Filling or creating food toys	✔	✔	✔	✔	**	✔	***
	Hide and seek game	✔	✔	✔	✔	**	✔	***
Play and games	Chase games with dangly toys	✔	✔	✔	✔	✔	✔	***
	Rolling balls for the cat	✔	✔	✔	✔	✔	✔	***
	Setting up independent toys for the cat	✔	✔	✔	✔	✔	✔	✔
Training	Sit	*	✔	*	*	*	✔	***
	Spin	*	✔	*	*	*	✔	***
	Entering a cat carrier	✔	✔	✔	✔	✔	✔	✔
	Target training	*	✔	*	*	*	✔	***

Figure 5.5. Some suggested activities for children to interact with cats, based on their individual differences. This is generic guidance and the selection of activities should be based on your discretion, the knowledge of the children and cat involved, and what is deemed suitable for them. Items marked with ticks should be fine to go ahead, while items marked with stars require some thought or preparation: a single star means activities can be carried out if the cat is calm and the interaction is supervised; two stars means carry out only after confidence building has been done with the cat; three stars means carry out only if the activities are not triggering for the cat.

provides guidance on a range of activities suitable for different family dynamics.

Relaxing

Encourage calm interactions with gentle strokes around the head, shoulders and back but not stroking from head to tail continuously as this tends to arouse cats. Most cats prefer gentle stroking around the head, base of the ears and shoulders, but be mindful of over arousal if more intense or thorough stroking is taking place. Make sure she is content with handling and if she has settled on your child's lap and is sleeping, try not to startle her or move too suddenly. If you

Cats and children can find comfort in relaxing near each other.

Brushing the cat is an activity that benefits both cats and children.

need to move her off your child's lap, gently wake her up first or gently lift her off your child's lap.

Some cats may seek out companionship and contact, but want very little physical touch. She may be content with sitting on a lap without being stroked or touched in any way, especially with an older child. It can be tempting in these situations to begin stroking the stomach or paws, especially if she is content and is exposing these areas. Children should be aware not to engage in stroking these areas as, for most cats, this will break trust. While the cat is settled, younger children could read to her or draw a picture of her. Any low noise activities whilst spending quality, positive time in her presence but with minimal direct interaction can help build confidence

The use of dangly toys can be fun for children and cats, as it encourages chase for the cat but will also keep the cat at a distance from the child's hands and feet. For young children it is best to supervise these interactions with excitable cats or consider alternative activities.

on both sides. Children will learn how to calmly interact with her, while she will gain trust that spending time with children can be relaxing and positive.

Some cats enjoy being brushed and other cats need to be brushed to prevent fur becoming matted. Therefore, this can also be a good activity for children to be involved in, making sure you supervise younger children.

Feeding and enrichment

Your children may have been assisting at feeding times and placing food into the cat's bowls since they were toddlers. As they grow up, they can start encouraging various games during feeding time and put food into food balls and puzzle feeders; which will not only provide fun for your child but also challenge your cat and encourage natural investigative type behaviours. These food toys don't have to be expensive products – you can encourage your child to get their creative heads on and design some food toys out of cardboard boxes, toilet rolls, etc.

The more confident cat may also like to seek out food in a game of 'hide and seek', very similar to scent work with dogs. Start by using your cat's favourite treat and encourage children to hide these in different places for the cat to find. Some may even enjoy searching through paper or boxes for treats, which is enriching for them but also fun for the children involved. Regular dry food can then be substituted in at mealtimes to increase activity and prevent boredom – it's an ideal game for indoor cats too.

Playing and games

Playing can be a time of high arousal for a cat, as mentioned in Chapter 1, therefore during times of play with children, you should use a variety of different toy like objects. The best types to use are the dangly toys, as these will offer both an extension of the arm and hand of the child but also elicit hunting-like behaviours from the cat, so are often the most favoured. Children should be taught from a young age not to use their hands and feet as play objects, especially with young kittens. An association between body parts and playthings can lead to injuries and distress for both parties.

Play sessions should be short to prevent over-arousal and/or frustration. Play should instigate positive feelings and therefore be tailored around the individual cat, their preferences and abilities. It may take some trial and error before truly understanding her preferences, especially if she is the new addition to the family. A range of toys and games can be practised to determine which she engages most in. Some cats prefer high energy chase games that replicate hunting behaviours, whereas others prefer more leisurely dabbing or passing games with various toys and balls.

Anything a cat deems frightening, aversive, or difficult and painful, will negatively impact the interactions between them and the child, which in turn impacts any form of relationship that is being built. It would be beneficial for the adults to determine her preferences prior to introducing these games with children, to ensure positive emotions from the offset. For cats that are easily aroused and can become a bit feisty, you can encourage your children to engage in less direct play by setting up toys that the cat can play with independently. Such toys could include automotive and mechanical toys that move independently and do not require input from a person. This enables the cat and child to experience play together, but in a safe and controlled way.

Training

Training is more likely to be undertaken by older children, however it is possible for younger children to get involved under supervision. This training can be used to encourage more appropriate behaviours as well as to increase the overall bond between child and cat. There are some key considerations to discuss with your child prior to undertaking any training so that they can undertake training effectively, including:

- Training sessions should be short and frequent, being carried out in 5-10-minute sessions because cats can quickly disengage. This will also avoid her getting too aroused and the training sessions becoming frustrating for her.
- You should consider which food treats are motivating for her and, where possible, use a variety to avoid her becoming fixated on one type, such as using a mixture of some lower value cat treats or standard kibble (if she will accept it) and high value treats such as fresh meat. Make sure food intake during meals is managed and exercise is encouraged where large amount of food rewards are needed. If training sessions are conducted frequently, it may be necessary to reduce the amount of food given at mealtimes, to balance the calorie intake.
- Always consider the cat's age and capabilities prior to any training sessions to ensure there are no welfare concerns.
- No punishment should be used during training and enough food treats should be provided to effectively establish the desired behaviours. Punishment negatively impacts relationships and should not be included with any interactions, especially those with children, as there is also a risk of injury.
- When providing food treats directly to her, try using tweezers or chopsticks so that she does not accidentally nip your fingers and mistake them for food. Alternatively, if she is not very impulsive and will not grab at your hands then you can lure with the food in your hands and then place the food on the floor to be eaten. These techniques will avoid bites and scratches, but younger children will need support with this, and parental supervision and guidance is always recommended.

Using chopsticks the child can move the food upwards over the cat's head to lure her into a sit position.

Using a food treat the child can lure the cat around in a circle.

The Sociable Cat

A few training exercises are described below including teaching the cat to sit (Exercise 12), teaching her to spin in a circle (Exercise 13), teaching her to enter a cat basket (Exercise 14) and teaching her to touch a target (Exercise 15). There are many more training exercises that you can perform with your cat, such as teaching her a recall, carried out in the same way that you would teach a dog, following Exercise 9 in Chapter 4.

Exercise 12: Teaching a sit

- With the food treat placed in tweezers or chopsticks, start with the food in front of the cat's nose.
- Lift the food up and over the cat's head until she is looking upwards, and her bottom is touching the floor. As she follows this lure say 'yes' and provide her with the food treat. Say 'yes' for every desired response immediately followed by the food treat.
- She may perform the sit in one go (with her bottom fully touching the floor) before you provide her with the food treat or you may need to learn the behaviour in stages, slowly getting her bottom closer and closer to the floor, for example first rewarding her as she looks upwards and her bottom moves towards the floor and then as she gets a little closer, etc. Do not reward her when she is reaching for the food with her paw.
- Keep doing this until she performs the full sit in one whole movement and then, if you want the behaviour to be on a verbal cue, you can start adding in a cue such as 'sit' before you lure her into the sit. You may need to keep luring her after you have provided the cue for a while, until she is performing the sit on the verbal cue alone, removing the lure altogether.

Top tips

- If she continuously tries to reach for the food with her paw, then move the food away from her and wait for her to put her paw down before starting again. Keep the food a bit closer to her nose while you lure her and ideally avoid providing her with any food while her paw is in the air.

Some cats like to climb legs or jump onto shoulders. This may be okay for older children if the cat does not get her claws out too much, but it is important to discourage this around young children.

Exercise 13: Teaching a spin

- With the food treat placed in tweezers or chopsticks start with the food in front of the cat's nose.
- Move the food around to her side and as she follows this lure say 'yes' and provide her with the food treat. Say 'yes' for every desired response immediately followed by the food treat.
- She may perform the whole spin in one go (spin in a 360 degree circle) before you provide the food treat or you may need to do the behaviour in sections, slowly getting closer to a full spin, eg first rewarding her as she turns a quarter of the way and then as she moves half way round, etc.
- Keep doing this until she performs the full spin in one whole movement and then, if you want the behaviour to be on a verbal cue, you can start adding in a cue such as 'spin' before you start. You may need to keep luring her after you have provided the cue for a while until she is performing the spin on the verbal cue alone.

Top tips

- If she is quite nervous and does not like you leaning over her it may be better luring from a standing position. However, this is very dependent on the individual. You may need to use higher value reinforcers and reinforce gradual movements to build her confidence with the task before you lean over her for the full spin.

Exercise 14: Entering a cat carrier

- Make sure the cat carrier has a cushion inside and is comfortable and then leave the cat carrier on the floor with its door open and with some of the cat's favourite treats placed inside.
- Every time the cat approaches the carrier, say 'yes', then provide her immediately with one of her favourite treats. Continue to do this every time she gets closer to the entrance of the cat carrier until she finally enters the carrier and gets the food treats from inside. While she is in the carrier make sure you keep the door open so that she can still exit by her own choice.
- Keep doing this and rewarding her while she sits in the carrier until she settles in there for longer periods. Only at this point should you shut the door but continue to drop some treats inside for her and only keep the door shut for a few seconds before opening it up again.
- Do this several times over a few days, making sure that she has a positive association of being in the carrier, but do not shut her inside for too long and always end the training sessions on a positive, leaving the door open for her so that she can choose to leave and end the session herself.

Top tips

- The cat may enter the carrier immediately or it may take time just encouraging her to approach, but this will be based on her past experiences around cat carriers and her level of confidence.
- You can use Exercise 2: Building confidence for further guidance about how to desensitise a cat to a stimulus that may be scary.

Exercise 15: Target training

- Decide what you want to use as the target – this can be anything you want the cat to touch, such as a target stick, an object in the room like a cup, a toy, or your hand. Be careful if using your hand, though, as if she becomes aroused or excited, she might scratch.
- Establish her preference for touch by considering how she investigates items. Most cats are likely to sniff objects, however if she is younger she may have a preference to use her paws. It is easier to train using a cat's own preference as she is more likely to offer up the desired behaviour.

- To begin training place the target in her view and as soon as she touches the target with her nose or paw say 'yes' and provide her with a food treat. Remove the target and then place the target back in view for her to do it again.
- Continue re-presenting the target and reinforcing her touching the target until she consistently performs the behaviour. Then as you present the target you can add in the verbal cue, such as 'touch' if you want to.

Some cats like to snuggle up really close, like this one, so make sure you're aware of their preferences and supervise them when around babies and toddlers.

TOP TIPS

- If she needs more encouragement, then you can lure her towards the target. If you want her to use her nose, then you can place food on or near the target to lure her nose towards it, and if you want her to use her paw then you can try placing a toy or ball near the target to lure her paw, although some cats may not engage with this.

5.5. Dynamics

It is important to continuously monitor the ongoing interactions and consider the safety of the children as well as the welfare of the cat. Some cats, particularly kittens and some specific breeds, like to interact in unique ways such as sitting on your shoulders or climbing up legs. So be aware of these unique preferences and behaviours and make sure that you are aware of these around younger children as they may get scratched. If these interactions are not preferred, focus on encouraging alternative interactions and watch out for indicators that she is likely to perform these behaviours and redirect, distract or engage in an alternative interaction prior to this. Be mindful that a young kitten climbing up legs or onto shoulders will very soon potentially be a 4kg+ cat, and the reactions to this behaviour will change drastically!

Behaviour is also likely to change over time as she ages. She may have different physiological and health considerations that affect interactions and how she perceives her environment, so make sure children are aware of possible changes in her behaviour due to factors such as pain, and teach them to adjust how they interact with her.

It is important for every child who encounters cats to receive guidance on how to interact with them. Additionally, interactions should be closely supervised, especially during the initial introductions to unfamiliar cats. Never assume a cat will be content with a range of different, and particularly unfamiliar, children just because she is fine with familiar children. If friends of children are coming around to the house, be mindful of your cat's personality and make sure she has the space away from them if she chooses not to interact with them.

It is normal for the occasional hiss, but where you feel she is continually or acutely stressed, is hiding a lot more or suppressing her natural behaviours and is rarely relaxed around the children, or if the children are getting scratched a lot, it is time to review progress. Either go back and start introductions from scratch, or complete further training for the cat and/or review the interactions between the children and the cat. Further training should be undertaken to increase the cat's confidence and/or further discussions may be required with your children. Consider alternative activities for them to do while the cat is around. Continue using positive reinforcement for desirable behaviours and to promote harmonious interactions, as well as manage arousal where necessary.

If you have concerns about the cat's welfare or behaviour, and you are noticing minimal progress in safely integrating her, or if her welfare is negatively impacted, ensure that you have thoroughly followed the introduction process and taken the necessary time to do so. If all stages have been undertaken slowly and with patience, going at the cat's pace, and/or the environment cannot be adjusted significantly to allow for better progression, then it would be beneficial to seek veterinary advice to rule out any potential health concerns that could be making the process less successful. At this point it would also be worth seeking advice from the cat's previous home, or getting support from an accredited behaviourist for further specialised advice for both new and existing cats.

About the authors

Melissa Fallon is a qualified and experienced clinical behaviourist and trainer. She gained her MSc in clinical animal behaviour at the University of Lincoln and has been in the education sector since 2009. Melissa has been teaching canine and feline behaviour and training, working specifically in higher education, as well as being involved in training cats for television. Melissa is also a mother of four humans, four felines and one canine. She is passionate about improving the welfare of felines in our society by understanding their behaviour better, and promoting safe and harmonious relationships between felines, canines and children.

Becky Macfarlane has worked in the education sector for 14 years and gained her MSc in Animal Welfare, Ethics & Law at the University of Edinburgh. She has experience lecturing in animal behaviour, welfare and ethics, more specifically teaching canine and feline specific content. She is also a trustee for a local feline charity, Band of Rescuers North Yorkshire, and has worked across various feline welfare charities over the last 20 years in varying capacities. Becky is also a mother of five humans, two felines and one canine, and is motivated to ensure harmonious relationships between all parties through promoting the need to understand human-animal interactions and responsible ownership. She has a passion for cats and ensuring they are better understood with regards to their behaviour, welfare and long-term outcomes in society.

Also by Melissa Fallon

With information and guidance on how to develop a safe and harmonious relationship between children and dogs, this book contains step-by-step exercises to prepare dogs to be around babies and children, help manage first interactions, teach children how to behave appropriately around dogs, and encourage positive relationships.

ISBN: 978-1-845848-90-3
Paperback • 20.5x20.5cm • 96 pages • 108 colour pictures
Ebook available

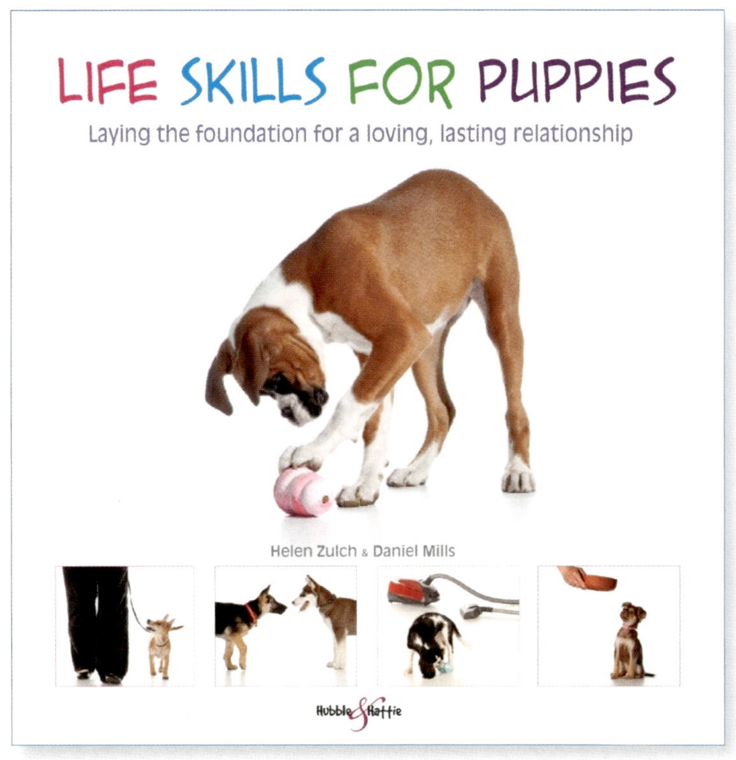

Puppy education from the puppy's perspective! This book presents key skills for dogs, helping owners to develop a fulfilling relationship with their puppy, while promoting good behaviour, resilience and welfare. Skills are incorporated into everyday life to reduce training time, so good manners and appropriate behaviour become a way of life.

ISBN: 978-1-787113-85-5
Paperback • 20.5x20.5cm • 96 pages • 121 colour pictures

Written by a qualified veterinarian, this is a comprehensive text that is highly relevant (even indispensable) to every dog and cat carer. Bursting with up-to-date information on all important areas of animal health, the information in this book will help maintain good health, or offer help and support during an illness.

ISBN: 978-1-787114-15-9
Paperback • 24x20cm • 224 pages • 58 pictures

Index